First World War
and Army of Occupation
War Diary
France, Belgium and Germany

9 DIVISION
1 Lowland Brigades
Headquarters
1 April 1919 - 25 September 1919

WO95/1776/1

The Naval & Military Press Ltd
www.nmarchive.com
Published in association with The National Archives

Published by

The Naval & Military Press Ltd

Unit 10 Ridgewood Industrial Park,

Uckfield, East Sussex,

TN22 5QE England

Tel: +44 (0) 1825 749494

www.naval-military-press.com

www.nmarchive.com

This diary has been reprinted in facsimile from the original. Any imperfections are inevitably reproduced and the quality may fall short of modern type and cartographic standards.

© **Crown Copyright**
Images reproduced by permission of The National Archives, London, England, 2015.

Contents

Document type	Place/Title	Date From	Date To
Heading	Lowland Division (Formerly 9 Division) H.Q. 1st Lowland Brigade (Late 26 Bde) 1919 Apr-1919 Sep		
Heading	War Diary of 1st Lowland Brigade Lowland Division Army Of The Rhine Volume 1 April 1919		
War Diary	Solingen Germany	01/04/1919	30/04/1919
Heading	War Diary for the month of May 1919 H.Q. 1st Bde		
War Diary	Solingen	01/05/1919	27/05/1919
Miscellaneous	Appendix No.1		
Miscellaneous	1st Lowland Brigade Defence Scheme		
Miscellaneous	1st Lowland Brigade Defence Scheme	30/04/1919	30/04/1919
Miscellaneous	Medical Arrangements		
Miscellaneous	Orders For Perimeter Posts No. 1 Sub-Area Lowland Division		
Miscellaneous	1st Lowland Brigade Defence Scheme Amendent No. 1	30/04/1919	30/04/1919
Miscellaneous	Advance Into Germany 1st Lowland Brigade Instructions No. 1	22/05/1919	22/05/1919
Miscellaneous	1st Lowland Brigade Instructions No. 2	25/05/1919	25/05/1919
Miscellaneous	Advance Into Germany Amendment To 1st Lowland Brigade Instructions No.2	27/05/1919	27/05/1919
Miscellaneous	1st Lowland Brigade Order No.289	27/05/1919	27/05/1919
Heading	Self Inflicted Injuries		
Heading	War Diary For Month Of June 1919 H.Q. 1st Low Bde		
Miscellaneous	Returns		
War Diary	Solingen	01/06/1919	18/06/1919
War Diary	Piepersberg	19/06/1919	28/06/1919
Miscellaneous	Ammendments and Addendum to 1st Lowland Brigade Instructions No.2	25/05/1919	25/05/1919
Miscellaneous	1st Lowland Brigade Order No.290		
Operation(al) Order(s)	Advance Into Germany 1st Lowland Brigade Order No.291	17/06/1919	17/06/1919
Operation(al) Order(s)	1st Lowland Brigade Order No. 292	18/06/1919	18/06/1919
Miscellaneous	Information And Instructions Regarding Railways In 1st Lowland Brigade Area	18/06/1919	18/06/1919
Operation(al) Order(s)	Advance Into Germany 1st Lowland Brigade Order No.288	18/06/1919	18/06/1919
Miscellaneous	Table To Accompany 1st Lowland Brigade Order No.288	17/08/1919	17/08/1919
Miscellaneous	Advance Into Germany 1st Lowland Brigade Instructions No.7	19/06/1919	19/06/1919
Operation(al) Order(s)	1st Lowland Brigade Order No.293	20/06/1919	20/06/1919
Miscellaneous	Advance Into Germany Amendment To 1st Lowland Brigade Instructions No.2		
Miscellaneous	Advance Into Germany	20/06/1919	20/06/1919
Operation(al) Order(s)	Advance Into Germany 1st Lowland Brigade Order No.294		
Miscellaneous	Message Form.		
Miscellaneous	Advance Into Germany 1st Lowland Brigade Instructions No.8		
Operation(al) Order(s)	1st Lowland Brigade Order No.296	26/06/1919	26/06/1919

Miscellaneous	March Table Issued With 1st Lowland Brigade Order No.296	26/06/1919	26/06/1919
Operation(al) Order(s)	1st Lowland Brigade Order No.295	26/06/1919	26/06/1919
Miscellaneous	Message Form.		
War Diary	Solingen Germany	01/06/1919	11/06/1919
Miscellaneous	Leave Return		
War Diary	Piepersberg	01/07/1919	01/07/1919
War Diary	Solingen	02/07/1919	10/07/1919
War Diary	Dormagen	11/07/1919	22/07/1919
War Diary	H S Arff	23/07/1919	31/07/1919
Miscellaneous	Distribution		
Miscellaneous	Move To Dormagen Area 1st Lowland Brigade Instructions No.1	08/07/1919	08/07/1919
Miscellaneous	Table "A"		
Miscellaneous	Table "B" Transport And Baggage Trains		
Miscellaneous	Distribution		
Miscellaneous	Move To Dormagen Area 1st Lowland Brigade Instructions No.1	08/07/1919	08/07/1919
Miscellaneous	Table "A" Personnel Train Table		
Miscellaneous	Table "B" Transport And Baggage Trains		
Operation(al) Order(s)	1st Lowland Brigade Order No.297	09/07/1919	09/07/1919
Miscellaneous	Table To Accompany 1st Lowland Brigade Order No.297	09/07/1919	09/07/1919
Operation(al) Order(s)	1st Lowland Brigade Order No.297	09/07/1919	09/07/1919
Miscellaneous	Table To Accompany 1st Lowland Brigade Order No.297	09/07/1919	09/07/1919
Operation(al) Order(s)	1st Lowland Brigade Order No.298	20/07/1919	20/07/1919
Miscellaneous	Move Of Brigade Headquarters From Dormagen To Hs Arff		
Operation(al) Order(s)	1st Lowland Brigade Order No. 298	20/07/1919	20/07/1919
Miscellaneous	Move Of Brigade Headquarters From Dormagen To Hs Arff		
War Diary	H.S. Arff	01/08/1919	16/08/1919
Operation(al) Order(s)	1st Lowland Brigade Order No.299	07/08/1919	07/08/1919
Miscellaneous	1/5th K.O.S.B	10/08/1919	10/08/1919
Miscellaneous	Allotment of Training Ground on The Dormagen-Neusz Road		
Miscellaneous	1/5th K.O.S.E.	21/08/1919	21/08/1919
Miscellaneous	Brigade Routine Orders by Brigadier-General G.T.C. Carter-Campbell C.B. D.S.O. Commanding 1st Lowland Brigade	26/08/1919	26/08/1919
Heading	1st Lowland Brigade Headquarters War Diary For September 1919		
War Diary	H.S. Arff	18/09/1919	25/09/1919
Operation(al) Order(s)	1st Lowland Brigade Order No.301	20/09/1919	20/09/1919
Operation(al) Order(s)	1st Lowland Brigade Order No.302	23/09/1919	23/09/1919
Operation(al) Order(s)	1st Lowland Brigade Order No.303	24/09/1919	24/09/1919
Miscellaneous	Special Order Of The Day	25/09/1919	25/09/1919

~~LOWLAND Res. 9 DIV~~

LOWLAND DIVISION (FORMERLY 9 DIVISION)

H.Q 1st LOWLAND BRIGADE
(LATE 26 BDE)

1919 APR — 1919 SEP

WAR DIARY

of

1st LOWLAND BRIGADE
LOWLAND DIVISION
ARMY OF THE RHINE.

oOo

VOLUME 1.   April, 1919.

Army Form C. 2118.

WAR DIARY
or
INTELLIGENCE SUMMARY.
(Erase heading not required.)

Instructions regarding War Diaries and Intelligence Summaries are contained in F. S. Regs., Part II. and the Staff Manual respectively. Title pages will be prepared in manuscript.

Place	Date	Hour	Summary of Events and Information	Remarks and references to Appendices
SOLINGEN Germany	April 1.		Instruction for Officers. Reference Action issued. Issue parade Educational Classes. Working parties on ranges. Weather dull.	Instruction for Off. 7th Victor. attd
	2		Issue parade Educational classes. Working parties on ranges. Weather dull.	attd
	3		G.O.C. visited right sector of the Left Battalion front in the morning & reconnoitred site for using in the afternoon. Attn. pointed out to the R3 and other officers concerned. Issue parades etc. Weather fine.	attd
	4		G.O.C. visited left sector of front reccod site for the using pointing it out to the R3 and other officers concerned. Weather fine.	attd
	5		Orders for the using of the Brigade Front issued. Issue parades etc. Weather fine.	attd
	6		Battalion attended Church service in the morning. Weather fine.	attd
	7		The using of the left portion of the right Battalion front commenced in the morning. In the afternoon the Divisional Commander visited Brigade Hqs & went over the Coal Steel factory Burgermeister in the evening.	attd
	8		The GOC visited the using parties on the left sector of the brigade front in	

Army Form C. 2118.

WAR DIARY
or
INTELLIGENCE SUMMARY.
(Erase heading not required.)

Instructions regarding War Diaries and Intelligence Summaries are contained in F. S. Regs., Part II. and the Staff Manual respectively. Title pages will be prepared in manuscript.

Place	Date	Hour	Summary of Events and Information	Remarks and references to Appendices
SOLINGEN Germany	April 8		the morning. Usual parades & training. Weather fine.	Cuil
	9		The G.O.C visited the wing on the right of the Left battalion front in the morning. 52nd Bn S.L.I. arrived from U.K. and joined the Brigade. Weather fine.	Cuil
	10		G.O.C. visited him in the afternoon. Usual parades. Weather fine. G.O.C. attended a conference at Bde H.Q. in the morning. Visited the 51 H.L.I. in the afternoon to make arrangements for their transfer to 6? Amalgamation with Bde H.Q.I. Usual parades. Weather fine.	Cuil
	11		G.O.C. attended a conference in the morning with officers of the Southern Division at MÜNGSTEN to discuss the lateup on of the postal KAISER WILHELM BRIDGE and MÜNGSTEN with our own troops. Conference Bde Major & Adjutants at Bde HQ in the afternoon. Weather had usual parades etc.	Cuil orders No 287
	12		G.O.C inspected transport of 51 H.L.I. in the morning. Usual parades. Weather dull	Cuil
	13		Battalions attended Church parade G.O.C inspected billets of J Coy MQ in the morning. Weather fine	Cuil
	14		G.O.C inspected preventive posts in the morning. The relief the 6/7/pol 67	Cuil

WAR DIARY
or
INTELLIGENCE SUMMARY.
(Erase heading not required.)

Army Form C. 2118.

Place	Date	Hour	Summary of Events and Information	Remarks and references to Appendices
	April			
SOLINGEN	14		2nd Lieutenant Bell carried out in accordance with Order no 287. Weather dull	CWR
Germany	15		Relief of Pols or Capt Offord in accordance with Order no 287. Completed stages of Sentries. Division holding them prisoner withdrawn. C p o	
			weather inspected rev pols. Horse parade, weather dull	CWR
	✗		Bde Major showed proposed cycling wire to Bde Major of 3rd Infant Brigade who followed the road to be taken over by them	
	16		Bde. Major TSC visited Adjutants. Horse parade etc. Fine	CWR
	17		GOC went to view HQ in the morning to 3rd Bde HQ at Bewark to discuss for difficulties of the civilian population with the Area Supervision. Horse parade. Sunday.	CWR
	18		GOC visited 3rd Bde HQ in the morning. Capt W Carlin transferred took over duties of Bde Major. Capt Pemberton to those of Staff Captain instead G.O.C visited K W Bridgehot in afternoon.	CWR
	19		Army Commander Sir Wm Robertson visited Divisional Area in the afternoon. Weather dull. GOC to town to meet the Army Commander	

Army Form C. 2118.

WAR DIARY
or
INTELLIGENCE SUMMARY.
(Erase heading not required.)

Instructions regarding War Diaries and Intelligence Summaries are contained in F. S. Regs., Part II. and the Staff Manual respectively. Title pages will be prepared in manuscript.

Place	Date	Hour	Summary of Events and Information	Remarks and references to Appendices
SOUCHEZ	Apr 2		Battalion attended Church Parades	
	" 3		Training continued. Tobe on Bm. holding the perimeter had not	W.L.
	" 30		returned to report.	
				Wants-Col M. S. O. returning Mole. H. Boulanger

Wt. W14422/M1160 350,000 12/16 D. D. & L. Forms/C/2118/14

ORIGINAL

WAR DIARY

FOR THE MONTH
OF
MAY 1919.
H.Q.
1st Bde

ORIGINAL.

WAR DIARY
of
1st Lowland Brigade
INTELLIGENCE-SUMMARY.

(Erase heading not required.)

for month of May 1919.

Army Form C. 2118.

Instructions regarding War Diaries and Intelligence Summaries are contained in F. S. Regs., Part II. and the Staff Manual respectively. Title pages will be prepared in manuscript.

Place	Date	Hour	Summary of Events and Information	Remarks and references to Appendices
Solingen	May 1/5/19		The locations of 1st Lowland Brigade on 1st May were as follows:-	
			Brigade Headquarters ⎫	
			15th H.L.I. ⎬ SOLINGEN.	
			1/5th K.O.S.B. ⎭	
			1st Lowland Brigade T.M.B.	
	1/5/19		51st H.L.I. on Outpost Duty on the perimeter with Head Quarters at SOLINGEN.	
			The Brigade Defence Scheme was revised and Copies issued to all concerned. Copy attached as appendix 1.	Appendix 1.
	17/5/19.		The Lowland Division Defence Scheme was amended regarding an advance into Germany and a conference was held at Divisional Headquarters on 18th inst at which the Brigadier and Brigade Major were present when the plans for this advance in the event of the German Delegates at VERSAILLES not signing the peace terms was discussed in detail. 1st Lowland Brigade Instruction No 1 were issued on 18th May.	Appendix 2.
	23/5/19		Lowland Division Order No 3 received. This order dealt with the Impending advance into Germany.	Appendix 3.
	25/5/19		Lowland Brigade Instructions No 2 issued.	Appendix 4.
	27/5/19		Lowland Brigade Order No 289 issued	

APPENDIX No I

Lowland Division.
1/5th K.O.S.B.
15th H.L.I.
51st H.L.I.
Brigade T.M.B.
50th Bde. R.F.A.

64th Field Coy. R.E.
105th Coy. R.A.S.C.
28th Field Ambulance.
9th M.G.C.
2nd Lowland Brigade.
3rd Southern Brigade.

No B.M.1/(b)/22   30th April 1918.

1.   Herewith Copy No...........of 1st Lowland Brigade Defence Scheme. This Scheme superseded the one previously issued, which will be returned.

2.   The Maps forwarded with the last Defence Scheme will be retained and affixed to this Copy.

3.   Please acknowledge receipt.

W. Carter
Captain,
Brigade Major,
1st Lowland Brigade.

COPY No...17......   SECRET

1st LOWLAND BRIGADE

DEFENCE SCHEME.

DISTRIBUTION

Copy No	1	G.O.C.
	2	Brigade Major.
	3	Staff Captain.
	4	Provost Officer
	5	Staff Captain (Civil Duties)
	6	Orderly Officer
	7	Lowland Division "G"
	8	Lowland Division "A"
	9	1/5th K.O.S.B.
	10	15th H.L.I.
	11	51st H.L.I.
	12	50th Bde. R.F.A.
	13	64th Field Coy. R.E.
	14	105th Coy. R.A.S.C.
	15	28th Field Ambulance.
	16	M.G. Bn. (For O.C. Company placed at disposal of Brigade Commander in cases of an emergen-cy)
	17	War Diary
	18	File
	19	2nd Lowland Brigade.
	20	3rd Lowland Brigade.
	21	O.C. Signal Section.
	22	Brigade T.M.B.

COPY No............

SECRET

1st LOWLAND BRIGADE
DEFENCE SCHEME.

1. The rule of the Lowland Division at present can be briefly summarised as follows:-

   (a) To guard and control that portion of the perimeter of the Bridgehead alloted to the Division.

   (b) Throughout the Divisional Area to maintain law and order and enforce the regulations laid down for the occupied territory.

   (c) To be in readiness to advance and occupy the Neutral Zone with or without fighting.

   (d) To protect the Divisional Sector against attack, and if forced to retire to fight a delaying action long enough to give time for supporting troops to cross the RHINE and occupy certain defended localities (shewn in RED on the attached Map).

2. The Divisional Area is divided into four Sub-Areas.

   No 1 Sub-Area is garrisoned by the undermentioned troops under the Command of the Brigade Commander, 1st Lowland Brigade:-

   1st Lowland Brigade
   50th Bde. R.F.A.
   64th Field Coy. R.E.
   105th Coy. R.A.S.C.
   28th Field Ambulance.

   In addition to the above one company (less half Company) 9th M.G. Bn is at the disposal of the Brigade Commander on emergency.

3. The boundaries of No 1 Sub-Area are shewn on attached map marked in RED, and indicate the limits of the Sub-Area as regards civil administration and accommodation. In addition, that portion of No II Sub-Area marked in PURPLE is alloted to the Brigade Commander No 1 Sub-Area for all tactical purposes.

ORDERS REGARDING THE HOLDING OF THE PERIMETER.

4. The Perimeter will be held by one Battalion with three Companies in the front line and one Company in Reserve in SOLINGEN.

    The following examining posts will be maintained:-

    RIGHT COMPANY H.Q. and three platoons (less 2 Sections) - SCHABERG.

        MUNGSTEN Post   1 Platoon.
        ELECTRIC WORKS Post   2 Sections.

    CENTRE COMPANY H.Q. and 3 Platoons - PAPIERMUHLE
        1 Platoon - ALTENB.U.

    finding:-

        PAPIERMUHLE Post   2 Sections.

    LEFT COMPANY H.Q. and three platoons (less 2 Sections)
    STOCKEN

        KOHLFURTHER Post   1 Platoon.
        WUPPER Post   2 Sections.

5. MUNGSTEN Post, PAPIERMUHLE Post and KOHLFURTHER Post will be under Command of an Officer, and a Union Jack will be flown at these posts and guard will be mounted with all due ceremony.

    Frequent patrolling will be carried out between all posts

    Sentries at all posts will pay proper compliments and guards will turn out under the normal regulations for guards.

ORDERS REGARDING THE MAINTENANCE OF LAW AND ORDER WITHIN THE SUB-AREA.

6. The following inlying picquets will be detailed by each Unit:-

    (a) The Battalion holding the perimeter, one platoon of each Company.
    (b) The remaining two Battalions, each one Company.
    (c) Other Units in the Sub-Area 25% of strength.

    These picquets will not remain under arms but must be ready to turn out armed and equipped, at short notice any time, day or night. 60 Rounds S.A.A. per Man will be held ready for issue so as to complete all men armed with a rifle to 120 rounds per man.

    Commanding Officers will arrange an alarm post for inlying picquets to fall in on, which is to be made known to all ranks.

7   The following system of Signals has been arranged for in the event of civil disturbance:-

A series of three short blasts given on certain selected factory hooters, and a series of three tolls sounded on certain Church Bells.

The selected Churches and Factories, and the Units with whom keys are deposited, are as follows:-

CATHOLIC CHURCH CRONENBERGER STRASSE   )
EGERSBERG and KRISCHBAUM, CRONENBERGER   ) 15th H.L.I.
STRASSE   )

PROTESTANT CHURCH, opposite Brigade H.Q.   ) Brigade Head-
T. HENKELS GUNERWALDER STRASSE   ) -quarters.

PROTESTANT CHURCH, KRAHENHOHE   ) 64th Field Coy R.E.
FACTORY DORST   )

The signals by hooters and Church Bells will be substituted by STROMBOS HORNS shortly.

18   This alarm Signal if given in one Sub-Area will be repeated in the other Sub-Areas.

The following action will be taken on this Alarm Signal sounding :-

    (a)   All Ranks who are away from their Units will immediately rejoin.

    (b)   All Guards will fall in on their Posts.

    (c)   The Guards mentioned in para 9 below will be immediately mounted.

    (d)   The inlying picquets will fall in on Alarm Posts.

    (e)   All Units will hold themselves in readiness to turn out fully armed and equipped.

8   On receipt of the message "PRECAUTIONARY ARRANGEMENTS" either by telephone or telegram the following action will be taken:-

    (a)   Inlying picquets will remain under arms in their Billets.

    (b)   The posts at MUNGSTEN and KOHLFURTHER will be doubled.

    (c)   All single sentries on the perimeter will be doubled.

    (d)   Guards as specified in para 9 below will be detailed.

    (e)   All troops will remain in the vicinity of their quarters.

    (f)   No passes will be granted without reference to Brigade Headquarters.

9. Battalions will be prepared to mount the following Guards:-

1/5th K.O.S.B.	1 N.C.O. and 6 Men	REICHBANK, 10 BIRKERSTRASSE.
Do	do	SPARKASSE BANK 23 SCHULSTRASSE.
Do	do	STOBBE BANK 11 WUPPERSTRASSE.
15th H.L.I.	do	DEUTCHE BANK 214 KAISERSTRASSE.
Do	do	MITTELDEUTSCHE BANK KAISERSTRASSE and BIRKERSTRASSE.
51st H.L.I.	do	BARMER BANK 22 KÖLNERSTRASSE.
Do	2 Sections	EXCHANGE, 54-56 KÖLNERSTRASSE.

All Units will mount Guards over Ammunition.

10. The Officer commanding the Battalion holding the Perimeter must be prepared at all times to hold the line of the perimeter against the incursion of an armed mob from REMSCHEID or ELBERFELD.

ACTION IN THE EVENT OF AN ADVANCE

11. The Area assigned to the Lowland Division is the area CRONENBERG - BARMEN - ELBERFELD - VOHWINKEL.

The 1st Lowland Brigade Group will move via CRONENBERG to BARMEN and will occupy the line - Bridge across the WUPPER on the LENNEP - SCHWELM road - DALHAUSEN - EHRENBERG - E. of LANGERFELD and BARMEN to road junction B 28, 98, exclusive, from whence the line will be continued by the 2nd Brigade.

ACTION IN DEFENSIVE OPERATIONS

12. The role of the Division is to fight a delaying action to give time for reinforcing troops to occupy the line of localities shown on map.

With this object in view the following line of resistance has been selected:-

The WUPPER RIVER from the MUNGSTEN BRIDGE to KOHL-FURTHER and from thence N. of RAUENHAUS to point G 41, 94 on the RAUENHAUS - GRÄFRATH Road.

13. The responsibility of holding this line will devolve on the Officer Commanding the Battalion holding the Perimeter.

In addition to his own Battalion the following troops will come under his Command:-

    2 Batteries 50th Bde R.F.A.
    1 Company 9th Bn M.G.C. (less half Company)

The nature of the Country and the extent of the front necessitate these batteries being employed by sections or even single guns. These positions are marked on map attached.

Eight alternative M.G. positions have been selected and are marked on attached map.

14. The following troops will be in Brigade Reserve and will not move without orders from Brigade Headquarters:-

    2 Battalions Infantry.
    2 Batteries 50th Bde R.F.A.
    1 Section 64th Field Coy. R.E.

The remainder of the 64th Field Coy. R.E. will come under the orders of the G.O.C.

15. In the event of the Brigade having to fall back a rear-guard action will be fought back to the line of defended localities mentioned in para 1 (d). The portion of this line to be held by the 1st Brigade is from UNTEN WIDDERT to KOHLSBERG. The line of retirement on to this position will be reconnoitred by all Units.

W. Carter
Captain,
Brigade Major,
1st Lowland Brigade,

SOLINGEN.
30th April 1919.

APPENDIX "A"

MEDICAL ARRANGEMENTS

1 Under Normal Conditions.

1. In normal times, as at present (April 22nd), evacuation of sick and all medical supervision in the 1st Lowland Brigade Group is carried out by the 28th Field Ambulance R.A.M.C., with Headquarters at EINTRACHT STRASSE, WALD.

II In Case of Active Operations.

2. LOCALITIES

   Regimental Aid Post.

       In the vicinity of Battalion H.Q. in the line.

   Advanced Dressing Station.

       Right   EINTRACHT STRASSE, WALD (F. 37,88)
       Left   SCHULESTRASSE, HILDEN (K. 39,57)

   Main Dressing Station.

       Hospital, OHLIGS (K 94,44)

   W. W. C. P.

       FESTEHALLE, OHLIGS (K. 83,48)

3. EVACUATION

   (a) **Lying Cases** From line of Defence to R.A.Ps by wheeled stretchers, thence by car to A.D. Stations car to M.D. station and tram or M.A.C. to C.C.S.

   (b) **Walking Cases** By returning vehicles, tramcars or H.A.W. to W.W.C.P. thence by train.

4. DUTIES OF FIELD AMBULANCES.

   27th Field Ambulance
       (1) M.D. Station.
       (2) W.W.C.P.
       (3) Evacuation from A.D. Stns.

   28th Field Ambulance
       (1) Evacuation of wounded from R.A.Ps near SOLINGEN and WALD.
       (2) Right A.D. Station.

   2/1st East Lancs. Field Ambulance.
       (1) Evacuation from R.A.Ps on h the front of the left Bde.
       (2) Left A.D. Station.

APPENDIX "A" (contd.)

5 On the outbreak of active operations, O.C., 28th Field Ambulance will attach 8 R.A.M.C. bearers to each R.M.O. of the Brigade, and Field Ambulance will at once assume the duties detailed in para 4.

6 CLERKING and A.T.S.

   Lying cases at M.D. Station.
   Walking cases at W.W.C,P.

APPENDIX "B"

ORDERS FOR PERIMETER POSTS.

No 1 Sub-Area, Lowland Division.

1   The sentries on duty at the perimeter posts will permit the following persons only to pass the posts:-

    (a)   Lieut-Col. STEWART, Second Army H.Q., Staff Officer, Neutral Zone.

    (b)   Major SCOTT-MURRAY, Second Army H.Q., Liason Officer, Section II, Neutral Zone.

    (c)   Staff Officers of Second Army Headquarters who may accompany the Officers mentioned in sub-para (a) and (b) above, and the chaffeur of the car driving the above Officers.

    (d)   Civilian persons holding a duly authorised pass and an identity card, the number on which should coinside with the number on the pass. Between the hours of 21.00 and 05.00 persons desiring to pass the posts must hold in addition to the above documents a night pass.
        Note.   Specimen day passes marked "A", "B" "C" and "D", identity card marked "E" and night pass marked "F" are already in possession of the Battalion finding the outposts and should be attached. These specimens will be handed over on relief.

    (e)   Persons entering the Occupied Area from the Neutral Zone who are in possession of a tele--gram from the Permit Office, D.P.M., Second Army, COLOGNE authorising them to enter the British Area, and, in addition a certificate from a Doctor to the effect that they are seriously ill and in urgent need of treatment in a Hospital at COLOGNE or BONN.

    (f)   Persons holding an Inter-Allied Railway Commission Passport, specimen of which marked "G" is already in possession of the Battalion finding the Outposts and should be attached.

2   In examining passes, sentries will pay particular atten-tion to the stamp and the date on which the pass expires, and will satisfy themselves that the bearer is the person indicated on the pass.

3   Sentries will permit no trams, motor cars, lorries or other vehicles of any kind to pass the posts until they have satisfied themselves that all occupants thereof come under one or other of the headings in para 1 above.

APPENDIX "B" (Continued)

4   Sentries will arrest:-

    (a) Any person, civil or military, British or German, who attempts to pass the posts in either direction, who is not provided for under one of the headings of para 1 of above.

    (b) Any persons, other than British Officers or soldiers, and the German Civil Police, bearing arms.

    (c) Any person behaving in a hostile manner towards or hindering them in the execution of their duty.

    (d) Any persons attempting to take out of the Occupied Area any foodstuffs of any kind without the necessary permit.

    (e) Any persons attempting to take out of the occupied area any raw material or manufactured articles for sale without the necessary permit.

    (f) Any persons attempting to evade the British Censorship Regulations by carrying in or out any uncensored letters, to or from persons in the Neutral Zone or the unoccupied area of Germany.

    (g) Any persons with whose names or descriptions they have been furnished from time to time for that purpose.

    (h) Any persons about whose bonn-fides they may have any doubt.

5   Any persons arrested by the sentries will be brought before the Officer in charge of the post, who, after satisfying himself that the persons should be detained, will despatch them under escort, together with a written report that any material or documentary evidence, to the Provost Officer at Brigade Headquarters.

6   No 5 Post has been selected as a point at which correspondence between British Military Authorities and the German Authorities will be exchanged.

A Cycle Orderly will be kept at the post for the purpose of delivering and correspondence to Brigade Signal Office twice daily, leaving the post for Brigade H.Q. at 11.30 and 16.00 hours. He will take back with him and correspondence for the Neutral Zone which will be delivered to the German Authorities at the post when called for.

Any correspondence passing either way marked "Urgent" will be forwarded S.D.R. - that _from_ the Neutral Zone by Cycle Orderly to Brigade H.Q. - that _for_ the Neutral Zone by a Brigade Signal Section orderly to the post.

APPENDIX "R" (Continued)

6 (Continued)

Correspondence for the Neutral Zone will usually be addressed:-

OBERST von POSER,
    ABSCHNITTS - KOMMANDEUR II,
        DER NEUTRALEN ZONE,
            WUPPERFURTH,
                RHEINLAND.

Any correspondence which does not appear to be official should be forwarded direct to Brigade H.Q. with a Report as to how it was delivered at the post.

G.O.C.	50th Bde. R.F.A.
Brigade Major.	64th Field Coy. R.E.
Staff Captain.	105th Coy. R.A.S.C.
Provost Officer	28th Field Ambulance.
Staff Captain (Civil Duties)	M.G. Battalion.
Orderly Officer.	2nd Lowland Brigade.
Lowland Division "G"	3rd Southern Brigade.
Lowland Division "A"	O.C. Signal Section.
1/5th K.O.S.B.	Brigade T.M.B.
15th H.L.I.	
51st H.L.I.	

No B.M./1 (b)/288   19th May 1919.

1st LOWLAND BRIGADE DEFENCE SCHEME DATED 30th April.
AMENDMENT No 1.

CANCEL Para 6 and substitute:-

    An inlying picquet strength 1 Company will be detailed by Units in accordance with weekly duty Roster published in B.R.Os.
    This picquet will not remain under arms but must be ready to turn out armed and equipped at short notice any time, day or night. 60 Rounds S.A.A. per man will be held ready for issue so as to complete all men armed with a Rifle to 120 Rounds per man.

ON RECEIPT of the MESSAGE
PRECAUTIONARY ARRANGEMENTS.

    Each Unit will form an inlying Picquet, from the men who are in Billets, until such times as the remainder of the men return to their quarters and can be paraded if required.
    Commanding Officers will arrange an Alarm Post for inlying Picquets to fall in on, which is to be made known to all Ranks.

PARA 9.   Add the following GUARDS.

        15th H.L.I.   1 N.C.O 6 Men   GLUDER PUMPING STATION.
        15th H.L.I.   1 N.C.O. 3 Men. RESERVOIR at KRAHENHOHE.

                                                Captain,
                                           Brigade Major,
                                         1st Lowland Brigade.

APPENDIX No 2   War Diary APPENDIX No 2.

Ref. MAPS
ELBERFELD } 1.25.000
BARMEN

SECRET

ADVANCE INTO GERMANY.

1st LOWLAND BRIGADE INSTRUCTIONS No 1

1. The Political situation may demand in the near future a further advance into Germany by the Allies.

2. Should such a move be ordered it may possibly be carried out at short notice, therefore these instructions are issued to give Battalion Commanders time to make the necessary arrangements.

3. **Surplus Stores.**

   Should an Advance be ordered all surplus kit and stores will be packed and stored as follows.

   15th H.L.I.
   51st H.L.I.   } at 51st H.L.I. Billet in
   1st Lowland Bde. T.M.B.   FREDERICK STRASSE.
   Brigade Headquarters.

   1/5th K.O.S.B.   at 1/5th K.O.S.B. Headquarters
                         SCHWERT STRASSE.

   The 51st H.L.I. will allot rooms in which the kit may be stored, a separate room will be alloted to each Unit. Each Unit will detail 1 N.C.O. and 1 Man to take charge of the stores.
   The transport of stores to Store Room will be done by Unit transport.
   Other Units of the Brigade Group will make their own arrangements for the storage of the kit.

4. **Battle Surplus.**

   The number of all ranks to move forward with 15th H.L.I. and 51st H.L.I. in the first instance will be as laid down in OB 1919 Page 8 Table 1V Columns 1 & 2.
   The 1/5th K.O.S.B. will leave behind not less than 10 Officers 2 N.C.Os and 24 Men. These will be furnished by the nucleus of the two Coys. who have not been made up for training purposes.
   The 1/5th K.O.S.B. will be organised in Headquarters and two Companies. The troops of 15th and 51st H.L.I. will be quartered in the 51st H.L.I. Billet in FREDERICK STRASSE. Those of the 1/5th K.O.S.B. in SCHWERT STRASSE.
   The senior Officer left at SOLINGEN will command all troops in the garrison, He will assume command from the time the head of the Brigade Column passes the starting point on the march forward. Name of senior Officer of each Unit and date of promotion will be wired to Brigade Headquarters as soon as the Officers to be left behind have been selected.
   As soon as troops are moved forward to take over the SOLINGEN AREA the personnel left behind by Units other than storemen and guards will be ordered by Brigade Headquarters to join their Units.

5. **Civil Administration.**

The Staff Captain, Civil Duties and Civilian Clerk will remain behind when the Brigade move and will continue his Duties until relieved by incoming Staff.

The Assistant Staff Captain and the Military Office Staff will move with Brigade Headquarters and will take over the Administration of the New Headquarters.

6. **Provost Arrangements.**

The Provost Officer will detail a few traffic Control men to remain in SOLINGEN until the rear guards leave the town. They will then join the rear Guards and march with them.

The remainder of Military Police and Traffic Control troops will march with Brigade Headquarters.

7. **Billetting Parties.**

If opposition to the advance is not expected to be met with the following billeting party will march with the Main Guard.

Brigade H.Qrs.	Civil Administration Officer. Orderly Officer and 4 Other Ranks.
1st Lowland Bde. T.M.B.	1 Officer 2 Other Ranks.
Each Battalion.	1 Do 5 Do
50th Bde. R.F.A.	1 Do 5 Do
28th Field Ambulance	1 Do 2 Do
105th Coy. R.A.S.C.	1 Do 2 Do
64th Field Coy. R.E.	1 Do 2 Do
Traffic Control	1 Do 2 Do

8. **Transport.**

Transport will march as follows:-
- Lewis Gun Limbers } With Companies.
- 1 Pack Animal }
- 1 Technical R.E. Cart.   With R.E. Section.
- 1 Signal Limber   With Brigade Signal Section.
- Maltese Carts
- Mess Carts
- Cookers and Cooks Limbers in the case of Units without Field Cookers.
- Water Carts

One Horse Ambulance as detailed by O.C. 28th Field Amb. will march with each Infantry Battalion.

The remainder of Transport will be Brigaded under the senior Transport Officer and march in rear of the Column. (rear Guard excepted) in the same order of march as their Units.

9. **Ammunition.**

Each man armed with a rifle will carry 120 rounds S.A.A.

10. The O.C. SOLINGEN Garrison will report to Brigade H.Qrs. for instructions as soon as he has been detailed for the duty.

11. These Instructions are for the information of Commanding Officers only. They will not be communicated to any one.

22/5/19.

W Carter Captain
Brigade Major 1st. Lowland Brigade

ADVANCE INTO GERMANY

APPENDIX No 3.

SECRET

REFERENCE MAPS
Sheets   GERMANY   2K 1;100,000
            ELBERFELD 1:25,000
            BARMEN   1:25,000

1st LOWLAND BRIGADE INSTRUCTIONS No 2

1   1st Lowland Brigade Instructions No 1 are hereby cancelled and will be destroyed.

2   In the event of the existing Armitice being terminated hostilities will recommence on J day after 72 hours warning.

The Allies then advance to seize the RUHR BASIN, the German railways essential for an advance, together with all rolling stock and German personnel for working the lines under our Orders.

The date of the probable J day will be communicated to all concerned and the exact hour and date of the advance will be notified in an Operation Order to be issued later.

3   The objective of the 1st Lowland Brigade Group is the occupation of the Area in which the following towns are situated:-

RONSDORF, BARMEN, LANGERFELD, SCHWELM, HASSLINGHAUSEN, GEVELSBERG, NAKSPROCKHOVEL, SILSCHEDE and ESBORM.

4   During the advance the Southern Division will operate on our right flank occupying REMSCHEID, RONSDORF and BARMEN on J day. Afterwards these troops move eastward and occupy SWERTE.
The 2nd Lowland Brigade will move forward on our left and occupy the line of the METTMAN-WULFRATH ROAD (exclusive)

The Belgians are advancing to the North of the BRITISH TROOPS the boundary being the METTMAN-WULFRATH-LANGENBURG-HATTINGEN-WITTEN ROAD. (Inclusive to the Belgians)

5   The following troops will compose the 1st Lowland Brigade Group.

        1st Lowland Brigade H.Qrs.
        1/5th K.O.S.B.
        15th H.L.I.
        51st H.L.I.
        1st Lowland Bde. T.M.B.
        C Battery 50th Bde R.F.A.
        1 Section 64th Field Coy R.E.
        A Coy 9th Bn M.G.C.
        1 Composite Cyclist Coy. (less 1 platoon)
        28th Field Ambulance.
        105th Coy. R.A.S.C.

6   The G.O.C. 1st Lowland Brigade will take over the command of the troops of 1/6th K.O.S.B. holding KLUSE, HOHE and LOOP POSTS on J - 2 days at 12 noon.

7   The Civil Administration of WALD and GRAFRATH will be taken over by 1st Lowland Brigade on J - 3 days. The Civil Administration of the 1st Lowland Brigade Area as held at 18.00 hours on J - 2 days will pass at that hour to the G.O.C. 2nd Highland Brigade.

8   Preparatory to an Advance Surplus Stores etc will be packed and stored on J day as follows.

    15th H.L.I.   at Battalion H.Qrs SCHUTZENBURG
    1/5th K.O.S.B. at Battalion H.Qrs SCHWERT STRASSE
    51st H.L.I.   )
    Brigade H.Qrs   ) at School Billet in
    Trench Mortar Battery) FREDERICK STRASSE.

Other Units of the Brigade Group will make their own arrangements for the storage of surplus kit. If accommodation is required, kit may be stored at 1/5th K.O.S.B. Headquarters and application should be made to that Unit. Storemen must be left in charge of such kits.

Each Unit will leave behind 1 N.C.O. and 1 Man as storeman. In addition the Battalions will leave behind 2 N.C.Os and 6 Men for Guard Duties on the Building in which the kit is stored.

It is expected that all kit left behind will be sent for after our new Area has been taken over. Guards and Storemen will act as baggage guard when the kit is brought along.

9   Battle Surplus will not be left behind.

10   The Provost Officer will hand over all traffic Control and Provost Duties to the incoming Brigade as 12.00 hours on J - 1 day.

11   The following billetting parties will be detailed for the advance.

    Brigade Headquarters.   Civil Administration Officer, Orderly Officer, Interpreter and 4 Other Ranks.

	Each Battalion	1 Officer	5 O.Rs
"C" Battery -	50th Bde R.F.A.	1 Officer	8 Other Ranks.
	1st Lowland Bde. T.M.B.	1 do	2 do
	1 Section 64th Field Coy R.Es.	1 do	2 do
	A Coy 9th Bn M.G.C.	1 do	2 do
	Cyclist Coy.	1 do	2 do
	28th Field Ambulance	1 do	2 do
	105th Coy R.A.S.C.	1 do	2 do
	Traffic Control & Police	1 do	2 do

These parties will march with the Main Guard unless otherwise ordered.

12   The Transport will march as follows unless orders are issued to the contrary.

    With Brigade H.Qrs   Cooks Cart
                                  Mess Cart
                                  1 Signal Limber.
    With Companies   Lewis Gun Limbers
                                  1 Pack Animal.
    With R.E. Section.   R.E. Techinal Cart.
                                  Cooks Limber.
    With Battalions.   Maltese Cart
                                  Mess Carts.
                                  Field Cookers.
                                  Water Carts.
                                  Remainder of Pack Animals.
                                  1 Horsed Ambulance to be detailed by O.C. 28th Field Ambulance.

12 (Continued)

The remainder of the transport will be Brigaded under the senior Transport Officer (Lieutenant J.N. MCHUGH)51st H.L.I.) and march in rear of the Column (rear Guard excepted) in the same order of March as their Units,

13. The dress for the advance will be Fighting Order as laid down in II Corps Letter G.T. 197 forwarded under this Office Letter B.M./8/175 of 9th May 1919. Each man armed with a Rifle except those specially detailed to carry 50 Rounds, will carry 120 Rounds S.A.A.

14. If available two lorries will be alloted to each Battalion to convey packs etc.
One lorry will be alloted to Trench Mortar Battery and one to Brigade Headquarters.

15. On J - 1 day Units of the 2nd Highland Division will relieve 51st H.L.I. and the two Coys. 1/6th K.O.S.B.'s on all perimeter posts.
Detailed Orders for the Relief will be issued later.

16. The Staff Captain (Civil Administration) will be responsible for the provision of Billets and for the allotment of the Billets to all Units in the Brigade Area. He will acquaint Units as early as possible of the billets assigned to them up to and including J - 1 day.
He will provide horse lines for incoming troops in the vicinity of their Billets.
He will prepare maps as early as possible showing the Billets and Horse Lines alloted to Troops on J - 3 J - 2 and J - 1.

17. Units will notify the Staff Captain (Civil Administration) of the number of Officers, Other Ranks and Animals for whom accommodation is required.
They will reconnoitre the Billets alloted and be prepared to occupy them at short notice.

18. Units vacating Billets will leave behind handing over parties if such Billets have been re-alloted to incoming troops. If no Troops are taking over the Billets will be closed. Staff Captain (Civil Administration) will arrange for the safe custody of requisitioned articles left in these Billets.
No requisitioned articles may be removed from the Billets. They will be handed over and receipts obtained in Duplicate, one copy being forwarded to Staff Captain (Civil Administration)

19. The Provost Officer will detail 9 men to act as guides to 2nd Highland Brigade on arrival. These guides will report to Brigade Headquarters at an hour to be notified later. They will be in possession of Maps of SOLINGEN.

20. The following moves will take place between J - 3 and J + 3 days both dates inclusive:-

J - 3 days

2nd Highland Brigade Group detrain at SOLINGEN and are billeted as follows:-

2nd Highland Bde. H.Qrs.	SOLINGEN.
A & B Bns.	SOLINGEN.
C Bn.	WALD.
2nd Highland Bde. T.M.B.	SOLINGEN.
1st Field Ambulance	SOLINGEN.

20 (Continued)

    1 Coy. Divisional Train.   SOLINGEN.
    1 Section R.E.   KRAHENHOHE
    Pioneer Bn. Highland Division.   SOLINGEN.

J - 2 days.

    1/5th K.O.S.B.   to   KETZBURG
    1st Lowland Bde. T.M.B. to   GRAFRATH.
    Composite Cyclist's Coy
       (less 1 Platoon)   to   GRAFRATH
    C Battery 50th Bde R.F.A. to   GRAFRATH.

J - 1 day.

    1st Lowland Bde. H.Qrs to   PIEPERSBURG North
                                       of GRAFRATH.
    A Coy 9th Bn. M.G.C.   to   GRAFRATH.
    28th Field Ambulance.   to   CENTRAL.
    105th Coy R.A.S.C.   to   OBEN FLACHSBERG
    1 Section 64th Field Coy R.E. to   GRAFRATH
    15th H.L.I.   to   GRAFRATH
    51st H.L.I. on Relief from Outpost
      Duty on Perimeter to Billets
      vacated by 15th H.L.I.
    X Southern Brigade Group to   SOLINGEN.
    16th H.L.I.   to   HAAN.
    63rd Bde. R.G.A. (less 1 Battery
      and one Section) to vicinity of HAAN & GRAFRATH

J Day.

    1st Lowland Bde. to VOHWINKEL & ELBERFELD and the
      high ground about points 303 and 291 (East of the
      VOHWINKEL - VELBERT ROAD)
    Brigade Headquarters   ELBERFELD.
    Battalion H.Qrs, 2 Coys Tank Corps to VOHWINKEL.

J + 1 day.

    No moves by Units of 1st Lowland Brigade Group.

J + 2 days.

    1st Lowland Brigade Group to objective described in
Para 3 taking over from Y Southern Brigade Group.

21   The following code will be employed to notify J
day to Units of 1st Lowland Brigade Group.
    PUNISH followed by figure or figures of the date
for example if J day is June 6th the following wire will
be sent out.

        PUNISH   6

On receipt of the above telegram the various preliminary
moves, reliefs etc laid down in these instructions will
commence from J - 3 day (June 3rd in above example)

21   The 2nd Highland Brigade will relieve the
following Guards now furnished by 1st Lowland Brigade
at 17.30 hours on J - 2 days.

Divisional H.Qrs	OHLIGS	1 Sergt., 1 L/Cpl 12 Men 1 Bugler and 1 Cook.
OHLIGS Railhead		1 Sergt 1 Corpl and 15 men.
104 Coy R.A.S.C.		2 N.C.Os and 10 men.
1st Lowland Brigade H.Qrs		2 N.C.Os and 6 Men.
105 Coy R.A.S.C. (Refilling Point)		2 N.C.Os 6 Men,

Each of the above Guards will send 1 N.C.O. as a Guide
to report to 1st Lowland Brigade H.Qrs ar 14.00 hours
on J - 2 days for instructions.

22   A Nominal Roll in duplicate will be rendered as
early as possible to Brigade Headquarters by all Units
of the Brigade Group of troops who are being left behind
in Solingen.   These men must be rationed by their own
Unit up to and for J + 2 days, After that day they will
be rationed by 2nd Highland Brigade.

Acknowledge.

War Diary

W. Carter
Captain,
Brigade Major
1st Lowland Brigade.

In the Field.
25-5-19.

DISTRIBUTION.

Copy No 1	G.O.C.
2	Brigade Major.
3	Staff Captain.
4	Staff Captain (Civil Administration)
5	Signal Officer.
6	Orderly Officer.
7	Provost Officer.
8	1/5th K.O.S.B.
9	15th H.L.I.
10	51st H.L.I.
11	1st Lowland T.M.B.
12	28th Field Ambulance.
13	105th Coy. R.A.S.C.
14	64th Field Coy. R.E.
15	50th Bde. R.F.A. for (C Battery)
16	9th Bn. M.G. Corps (for A Coy.)
17	Composite Cyclist Coy.
18	Lowland Division "G"
19	Lowland Division "Q"
20	2nd Lowland Brigade.
21	3rd Lowland Brigade.
22	2nd Highland Brigade.
23	~~3rd~~ Southern Division for X Brigade.
24	~~4th~~ Southern Division for Y Brigade.
25	16th H.L.I.
26	53rd Bde R.G.A.
27	Tank Battalion.
28	File Copy.
29 & 30	War Diary.
31, 32, 33	Spare.

ADVANCE INTO GERMANY.

AMENDMENT to 1st LOWLAND BRIGADE INSTRUCTIONS No 2
dated 25th MAY 1919.

Amendment No 1

Para 8 line 2 for "on" read "before"

Amendment No 2

Cancel Para 12 and substitute.
The Transport will march as follows unless orders to the contrary are issued:-

With Coys. of the Advance Guard,	Lewis Gun Limbers 1 Pack Animal. Field Cookers.
With other Coys.	Lewis Gun Limbers. 1 Pack Animal.
With Units.	Remainder of Transport not with Coys. 1 Horsed Ambulance.

One horsed Ambulance will accompany each Battalion. The O.C. 28th Field Ambulance will detail these to Units.

Amendment No 3.

Para 14 add:-
The lorries conveying the baggage will be loaded up and will rendezvous at KLUSE POST at ZERO + 2.30 hours on J day. Capt. McNaughton Brigade Education Officer will be in charge of Motor Lorries on the March.

Amendment No 3.

Add new para.
23 The 2nd Highland Brigade will relieve the undermentioned employ on J - 2 days.
    Y.M.C.A. Canteen   3
    Salvation Army Canteen   3
    Scottish Churches Hut   6

The men relieved will rejoin their Unit.

Distribution to all recipient of Instructions No 2.

W. Carter
Captain,
Brigade Major,
1st Lowland Brigade.

27-5-19.

APPENDIX No 4 **SECRET**

ADVANCE INTO GERMANY

Reference Map.
Solingen Sheet.
1/25,000

1st LOWLAND BRIGADE ORDER No 289

1. The following moves will take place on J - 2 day. J day will be communicated later.

    (a) The 1/5th K.O.S.B.   Solingen to KETZBURG
    (b) 1st Lowland Bde T.M.B.   to GRAFRATH
    (c) "C" Battery 50th Bde R.F.A.   to GRAFRATH

2. Unit Commanders will arrange their own hour of march.

1/5th K.O.S.B. will be clear of the Cross Road Junction of KAISER STRASSE and KRONPRINZ STRASSE by 10.00 hours.
"C" Battery 50th Bde. R.F.A. will not cross the Railway Bridge SCHUTZEN STRASSE before 10.00 hours.
Move to be completed by 12.00 noon.

3. Location of new Headquarters will be wired to Brigade Headquarters immediately after occupation.

4. Lorries will report to Unit Headquarters at 07.30 hours on J - 2 days.

5. Acknowledge.

                             W. Carter,
                             Captain,
                         Brigade Major,
27-5-19.   1st Lowland Brigade.

DISTRIBUTION

Copy No 1. G.O.C.
       2 Brigade Major.
       3 Staff Captain.
       4 Staff Captain (Civil Administration)
       5 Signal Officer.
       6 Provost Officer.
       7 1/5th K.O.S.B.
       8 15th H.L.I.
       9 51st H.L.I.
     10 1st Lowland Bde. T.M.B.
     11 28th Field Ambulance.
     12 105th Coy R.A.S.C.
     13 "C" Battery 50th Bde R.F.A. (thro 50th Bde.R.F.A.)
     14 Lowland Division "G"
     15 Lowland Division "Q"
     16 2nd Highland Brigade.
     17 File
     18 & 19 War Diary.
     20, 21 & 22 Spare.

(6339) Wt. W160/M3016 1,500,000 10/17 McA & W Ltd (E 1898) Forms W3091.   Army Form W.3091.

Cover for Documents.

Nature of Enclosures.

SELF·INFLICTED·INJURIES

Notes, or Letters written.

Original.

HQ
1st Low Bde

War Diary
for
Month of June 1919

Returns

ORIGINAL

Army Form C. 2118.

WAR DIARY 1st June 1919.

INTELLIGENCE SUMMARY

(Erase heading not required.)

Instructions regarding War Diaries and Intelligence Summaries are contained in F. S. Regs., Part II. and the Staff Manual respectively. Title pages will be prepared in manuscript.

Place	Date	Hour	Summary of Events and Information	Remarks and references to Appendices
Solingen	1st June		On 1st June 1919 1st Lowland Brigade was quartered as under:-	
			Brigade Headquarters SOLINGEN	
			1st Lowland Brigade Trench Mortar Battery	
			1/5th K.O.S.B.	
			15th H.L.I.	
			51st H.L.I. in the line holding the perimeter	
			The 1/5th K.O.S.B. were continuing the training of N.C.Os and skeleton Sections being very weak as regards numbers.	
			15th H.L.I. carried out the training of Instructors from 1st to 14th June and from then till end of the month has been alloted to Section and Platoon training.	
	17th		Amendment No 5 to 1st Lowland Brigade Instructions No 2 issued (Advance into Germany)	Appendix A
	"		1st Lowland Brigade Order No 290 dated 17.6.19 issued (move to assembly Area)	" B
	"		1st Lowland Brigade Order No 291 dated 17.6.19 issued (relief of 51st H.L.I. in the line)	" C
	"		1st Lowland Brigade Order No 292 dated 18.6.19 issued (relief of 1/6th K.O.S.B. in the line)	" D
	18		Information and Instructions regarding Railways in 1st Lowland Brigade Area (Elberfeld) issued	" E
	1st L			

ORIGINAL

Army Form C. 2118.

WAR DIARY 1st June 1919.

INTELLIGENCE SUMMARY

(Erase heading not required.)

Instructions regarding War Diaries and Intelligence Summaries are contained in F.S. Regs., Part II. and the Staff Manual respectively. Title pages will be prepared in manuscript.

Place	Date	Hour	Summary of Events and Information	Remarks and references to Appendices
Solingen	18th June		1st Lowland Brigade Order No 288 dated 18th June for the march into Germany on 2 day issued.	Appendix F
PIEFERSBERG	19th		Brigade Group moved to assembly Area preparatory to the Advance into Germany and were located as follows:-	
			Bde. Headquarters PIEFERSBERG	
			15th H.L.I. GRAFRATH.	
			1st Lowland Bde. T.M.B. CENTRAL	
			8th Corps Cyclist Bn. GRAFRATH.	
			1/5th K.O.S.B. KETZBERG	
			105th Coy. R.A.S.C. CENTRAL	
			'A' Bty. 50th Bde R.F.A. FLASHBERG	
			'A' Coy 9th Bn. M.G.C. CENTRAL	
			51st H.L.I. North part of SOLINGEN.	
			28th Field Ambulance CENTRAL	
	19		1st Lowland Bde. Instructions No 2 dealing with notification of J day and Policy as regards use of Artillery Projectiles issued	Appendix G
	20		Brigade Order No 293 dated 20.6.19 issued (move of 51st H.L.I.)	" H
	"		Amendments to Instructions No 2 issued	" I
	"		Amendments to 1st Lowland Brigade Order No 288 dated 18.6.19 issued	" J
	"		1st Lowland Brigade Order No 294 dated 23.6.19 issued. (Zero hour and date of Advance.)	" K
	23		Brigade Telegram No S.O. 96 dated 23rd June 1919, notifying Units that Germany would sign	

ORIGINAL

Army Form C. 2118.

WAR DIARY 1st June 1919.
INTELLIGENCE SUMMARY.
(Erase heading not required.)

Instructions regarding War Diaries and Intelligence Summaries are contained in F.S. Regs., Part II. and the Staff Manual respectively. Title pages will be prepared in manuscript.

Place	Date	Hour	Summary of Events and Information	Remarks and references to Appendices
PIEPERSBERG	23rd June		the Peace Terms and that no Advance would be made.	Appendix L
	"		1st Lowland Bde. Instructions No 8 dealing with the Garrisoning and Defence of ELBERFELD after occupation by our troops issued 23.6.19.	" M
	26th		Brigade Order No 296 ordering the return of the Brigade Group to SOLINGEN AREA at a date to be notified later issued.	" N
	"		Brigade Order No 295 order 51st H.L.I. to relieve 51st Gordon Highlanders in the line at a date to be notified later issued.	" O
	28th		Information received at 19.00 that the Peace had been signed and that moves back to SOLINGEN would commence on 30th June.	" P
	1/7/19.			

[signature]
Brigadier General,
Commanding 1st Lowland Brigade.

A   Appendix
                                                            A

ADVANCE INTO GERMANY

AMMENDMENTS and ADDENDUM to 1st LOWLAND BRIGADE

INSTRUCTIONS No 2 dated 25th May 1919.

Ammendment No 5.

Add to Para II
All Billeting Parties will report to Captain Cave, Brigade Musketry Officer at places and times as will be notified later and will be marched by that Officer in a formed body immediately in rear of the Infantry of the Main Guard.

Cancel Para 18 and substitute.
18. Units vacating Billets will leave behind handing over parties if such Billets have been re-alloted to incoming troops. If ho Troops are taking over, the billets will be handed over to the owners. If the owners cannot be found the billet will be locked up and the key handed to Staff Captain (Civil Administration)

No requisitioned articles may be removed from the billets. They will be collected and stored in the Unit Storeroom. Large articles such as beds, tables and forms will be left in the billets and a list showing billet address will be forwarded to the Staff Captain (Civil Administration)

Para 20
Opposite "C" Battery for GRAFRATH read OBEN FLASCHEND
Opposite 1st Lowland T.M.B.   ) for GRAFRATH
        "A" Coy. 9th M.G.C.   )
        1 Section 64th Field Coy. R.E.) CENTRAL AREA.
    Last line after the word and figure "para 3" add except the towns of SCHWELM and GEVELSBERG. After the word group, in same line add J + 3 days, take over SCHWELM and GEVELSBERG.

Add new paras.
24. Ground Sheets and Strips will always be displayed at Report Centres of Brigade and Battalion H.Qrs and Report Centres when at the halt.
The sites on which the Strips are exposed must be in the open so that they can be easily seen from the air.

25. Copies of Proclamations will be posted up in all towns and villages in the Brigade Area.
These will be put up by a Party of 1 N.C.O. and 2 men to be detailed by the Provost Officer.
This Party will accompany the most advanced troops and the Proclamations will be put up immediately after the troops enter the Towns or Villages.
The Staff Captain (Civil Administration) will requisition a Motor Car at SOLINGEN and allot it to the Provost Officer for this purpose.
Copies of Proclamations, Paste tins, Brushes and Flour will be issued to Provost Officer on J - 1 day.

26 Copies of 4 Letter Code Calls will be issued to Units on J - 1 day. Receipt of same will be acknowledged.

- 2 -

27. SUPPLIES

Beginning on the first day that Units move, rations will be delivered by No 2 Coy. Divisional Train.

28. BAGGAGE WAGGONS
will report to Units at 07.00 on first day that Units move. They will return to No 2 Coy. Divisional Train on the evening of J + 3 day.

29. IRON RATIONS

Iron Rations will be issued from Re-Filling points on J - 1 day to complete the scale of 1 Iron Ration per man.

30. AMMUNITION

Indents for Ammunition will be forwarded to Brigade Headquarters. S.A.A. Section D.A.C. will deliver ammunition to Units Transport Lines on receipt of written Authority from Brigade Headquarters. S.A.A. Section will move to VOHWINKEL on J day.

31. PERSONNEL and RECEPTION CAMP

The Divisional Reception Camp will remain at OHLIGS until Personnel Railhead moves.
All men proceeding on leave will pass through the Reception Camp in the ordinary way and will proceed thence via the Surplus Stores Dump where they will pick up their rifles etc before proceeding to join their Units.

32. ORDNANCE

D.A.D.O.S. has arranged to maintain a reserve of Box Respirators M.C. Containers, Lewis Guns and spare parts for Lewis Guns.

33. VETERINARY

(a) No stable should be taken over and used in the New Area until it has been thoroughly disinfected under the direction of a Vetinary Officer or his representative.
All Animals should be picketed in the open until this has been done.
(b) No wooden water troughs, hayracks or mangers shall on any account be used. There is no objection to the use of those made of iron providing they have been thoroughly disinfected.
(c) Animals should not be watered from wells. Running streams are always preferable, buckets should be used until suitable troughs are available.
(d) No civilian forges may be used. Animals should be shod in their own lines.

34 FEEDING OF CIVILIANS.

If inhabitants in the territory about to be occupied are found to be without food they will be fed on a basis of 1 British ration to 4 adults. Staff Captain Civil Administration will notify Brigade Supply Officer direct of the number of rations required.

Not more than 100 may be fed without reference to Divisional Headquarters. The feeding of large numbers will be arranged by General Headquarters.

35 REPORTS.

The following reports will be rendered from J day and daily afterwards by Battalions to Brigade Headquarters.

(a) Morning Situation Report.
Daily (by wire if possible) so as to reach Brigade Headquarters by 05.30 hrs.

(b) Evening Situation Reports (including Prisoners of War and material captured)
Daily (by wire if possible) so as to reach Brigade Headquarters by 14.30 hrs.

(c) Location of Battalion Headquarters as they will be at 06.00 hrs. on the following day.
BY D.R.L.S. so as to reach Brigade Headquarters not later than 12.00 hrs.
To be rendered from J - 3 days onwards.

(d) Return of Prisoners Captured
BY Priority Wire giving Unit of Prisoners, as soon as possible after capture.

(e) Daily Intelligence Summaries for period from 20.00 to 20.00 hrs. These will be forwarded:-
From period 20.00 hrs. to 15.00 hrs. by 16.00 hrs.
"   "   15.30 hrs. BY wire or telephone immediately after 20.00 hrs.

36   G.S. 1b personnel are accompanying advanced guards and are responsible for seizing suspects in the area to be occupied. When demanded guards will be furnished.

ADVANCE INTO GERMANY.

1st LOWLAND BRIGADE ORDER NO 290.

Reference Maps.

Germany 2K 1/100000
Germany 2S.N.W. 1/25000

17.6.19.

1. Moves in accordance with attached table will take place on 19th June 1919.

2. Units will move independently.

3. Completion of march and location of new Headquarters will be wired to Brigade Headquarters immediately after arrival at destination.

4. Lorries will report at Unit Headquarters at 07.30 hours on 19th inst.

5. Brigade Headquarters will close at SOLINGEN at 10.00 hrs. and re-open at PIEPERSBURG at the same hour.

Acknowledge.

W Carter
Captain.
Brigade Major
1st Lowland Brigade.

Serial No	Unit	Starting Point	Hour of Passing	Route
1	154th L.I.	Road and Railway Crossing. F 4372	08.00 hours	CENTRAL GRAFRATH ROAD.
2	Field Ambulance	Do	08.15 hours	Do Do
3	105 Coy R.A.S.C.	Do	08.30 hours	SOLINGEN GRAFRATH ROAD
4	1 Section 64th Field Coy. R.E.	Do	09.00 hours	Do Do
5	1st Lowland Bde, H.Qrs.	Do	10.00 hours	Do Do
6	"A" Coy 9th M.G.Bn	To march under own arrangement. To reach CENTRAL by 13.00 hours.		

DISTRIBUTION

Copy No 1   G.O.C.
       2   Brigade Major.
       3   Staff Captain.
       4   Staff Captain (Civil Administration.)
       5   Signal Officer.
       6   Orderly Officer
       7   Provost Officer
       8   1/5th K.O.S.B.
       9   15th H.L.I.
       10   51st H.L.I.
       11   1st Lowland Brigade T.M.B.
       12   23th Field Ambulance.
       13   Section 64th Field Coy. R.E.
       14   "A" Battery 50th Bde. R.F.A.
       15   "A" Coy 9th M.G.Bn.
       16   Composite Coy. 8th Cyclist Battn.
       17   Lowland Division "G"
       18   Lowland Division "Q"
       19   2nd Lowland Brigade.
       20   1st Lowland Brigade.
       21   2nd Highland Brigade.
       22   65rd Brigade R.D.A.
       23 & 24 War Diary.
       25, 26 & 27 Spare.
       28   File Copy.

Appendix. C

ADVANCE INTO GERMANY.

1st LOWLAND BRIGADE ORDER No. 291.

Reference Map,
SOLINGEN.
                                                                        17th June, 1919.

1.   The 51st H.L.I. will be relieved in the line on 19th June, 1919, by the 51st Battn. Gordon Highlanders.

2.   The details of relief will be arranged by Battalion Commanders direct.

3.   All order boards, Instructions, and copy of Defence Scheme will be handed over on relief. Stores held on charge at the Outposts will also be handed over and receipts obtained.

4.   51st H.L.I. will leave behind with the incoming Unit one officer per Company and one N.C.O. per post. This personnel will rejoin their Battalion after 18.00 hours same date.

5.   On relief 51st H.L.I. will move into SOLINGEN and take over the accommodation vacated by the 15th H.L.I.

6.   Completion of relief to be wired to Brigade Headquarters.

    Acknowledge.

W Carter
Captain,
Brigade Major,
1st Lowland Brigade.

DISTRIBUTION

Copy No	1	G.O.C.
	2	Brigade Major.
	3	Staff Captain.
	4	Staff Captain (Civil Administration.)
	5	Signal Officer.
	6	Orderly Officer
	7	Provost Officer
	8	1/5th K.O.S.B.
	9	15th H.L.I.
	10	51st H.L.I.
	11	1st Lowland Brigade T.M.B.
	12	23th Field Ambulance.
	13	Section 64th Field Coy. R.E.
	14	"A" Battery 50th Bde. R.F.A.
	15	"A" Coy 9th M.G.Bn.
	16	Composite Coy. 8th Cyclist Battn.
	17	Lowland Division "G"
	18	Lowland Division "Q"
	19	2nd Lowland Brigade.
	20	1st Lowland Brigade.
	21	2nd Highland Brigade.
	22	63rd Brigade R.F.A.
	23 & 24	War Diary.
	25, 26 & 27	Spare.
	28	File Copy.

Appendix "D"

1st. LOWLAND BRIGADE   ORDER No. 392.

Reference Maps.
Germany 2 S.W. 1/25,000   18TH June 1919.

1. The 1/5th. K.O.S.B. (2nd. Lowland Brigade) will be relieved in the line by 4th. Bn. Gordon Highlanders 2nd. Highland Division on 19th. June 1919.

2. All arrangements for relief to be made between Unit Commanders direct.

3. The posts held by the 1/5th. K.O.S.B. and strength of garrison are given below.

				Off.	O.Rs.
No 1	KIUSE	POST	A3614	4	54
No 2	HOHE	POST	A2609	-	10
No 3	LOOP	POST	A1209	3	55

4. All order boards, instructions and copy of Defence Scheme will be handed over on relief.
   Stores held on charge of posts will also be handed over and receipts obtained.

5. 1/5th K.O.S.B. will leave behind with the incoming unit one officer at KIUSE POST, one officer at LOOP and 1 N.C.O. at HOHE This personnel will rejoin their unit at 1800.

6. On completion of relief 1/5th. K.O.S.B. will revert to the command of 2nd. Lowland Brigade.

7. The Command of the troops holding the perimeter will pass to the G.O.C. 2nd. Highland Brigade at 10 hours on 19th. June 1919.

Captain,
Brigade Major,
1st. Lowland Brigade.

DISTRIBUTION.

```
Copy No 1.     G.O.C.
        2.     Brigade Major.
        3.     Staff Captain.
        4.     Staff Captain (Civil Administration.)
        5.     Signal Officer
        6.     Orderly Officer.
        7.     Provost Officer.
        8.     1/5th K.O.S.B.
        9.     15th H.L.I.
       10.     51st H.L.I.
       11.     1st Lowland Brigade T.M.B.
       12.     28th Field Ambulance.
       13.     Section 34th Field Coy. R.E.
       14.     "A" Battery 50th Bde. R.F.A.
       15.     "A" Coy. 9th M.G. Bn.
       16.     Composite Coy. 8th Cyclist Battn.
       18.     Lowland Division "G"
       18.     Lowland Division "Q"
       19.     2nd Lowland Brigade.
       20.     3rd Lowland Brigade.
       21.     2nd Highland Brigade.
       22.     63rd Bde. R.G.A.
       23.     105th Coy. R.A.S.C.
       24. & 25 War Diary.
       26,27 & 28. Spare.
       29.     File Copy.
       30.     1/6th K.O.S.B.
```

Appendix E

SECRET.

ADVANCE INTO GERMANY.

Reference Maps.
  Germany 2 K 1/10,000
           2 S.N.W. 1/25,000

INFORMATION and INSTRUCTIONS regarding RAILWAYS in 1st LOWLAND BRIGADE AREA.

1. One of the principal objectives of the first stage of the Advance is to secure complete control over the German Railways Systems that are considered essential for a further advance.

2. The Railways in 1st Lowland Brigade Area is the VOHWINKEL - BARMEN - ELBERFELD - SCHWELM & GEVELSBERG Railways which runs through these towns and the loop line which runs from VOHWINKEL North of ELBERFELD and BARMEN.

3. As far as can be ascertained from the map the following railway Bridges, Tunnels and Junctions will require to be guarded or patrolled.

    (1) Road and Railway Bridge.   at   A 61 57
    (2)   "   "   "   "   A 64 59
    (3) Tunnel   "   A 67 61
    (4)   "   "   A 71 62
    (5) Road and Railway Bridge.   "   A 73 62
    (6)   "   "   "   "   A 78 65
    (7)   "   "   "   "   A 79 65
    (8) Tunnel.   "   A 94 59
    (9)   "   "   A 95 58
    (10) Road and Railway Bridge.   "   A 78 45
    (11)   "   "   "   "   A 86 50
    (12)   "   "   "   "   A 95 53
    (13)   "   "   "   "   A 05 55

It will be necessary for Units to patrol the whole of the lines within their Area to verify the above information and to ascertain if any other important Bridges, Tunnels etc exists.

4. The responsibility for guarding the railway system other than that for which guards are detailed in Para 9 of 1st Lowland Brigade Order No 238 of today's date is as follows:-

  1/5th K.O.S.B.   Railways in Squares A 66, 65, 76, 75, 64, and 74 except Bridges at A 78.64 and A 79.65 and railways between these Bridges.
  15th H.L.I.   Bridges at A 78.64, A 79.65 and A 62.65 and railway between these Bridges.
  51st H.L.I.   Railways in Squares A 65 (except between Bridges A 79.65 and A 62.65) 96, 95, 85 and 84.

5. Any damage done to German lines is to be purely temporary (i.e. by breaking a rail in one or two places), this only to be done in case of withdrawal, in order to prevent the circulation of German trains whilst awaiting the resumption

6. The control of the General Management of the Railways will be taken over by a SOUS-COMMISSION of the C.I.C.F.C. A Railway Liaison Officer has been appointed and he will be located at ELBERFELD. The Liaison Officer, together with the necessary Railhead Staff and Railway Police will accompany the advanced troops.

7. After the SOUS-COMMISSION have taken the Railways over (of which notice will be given to Units) Unit Commanders will ensure that:-
   (a) No Railway working is interfered with and no railway Officials are molested or interfered with in their work. In the first instance, these Railway Officials will have no passes, but they will be provided with them by the SOUS-COMMISSION as early as practicable.
   (b) No Railway telephones or telegraphs are interfered with, as they are vital to the continued working of the line.
   (c) No Railway Buildings or premises are commandeered or occupied without reference to Brigade Headquarters.

18/6/19.

Butler
Captain,
Brigade Major,
1st Lowland Brigade.

DISTRIBUTION.

Copy No 1.   G.O.C.
- 2. Brigade Major.
- 3. Staff Captain.
- 4. Staff Captain (Civil Administration.)
- 5. Signal Officer
- 6. Orderly Officer.
- 7. Provost Officer.
- 8. 1/5th K.O.S.B.
- 9. 15th H.L.I.
- 10. 51st H.L.I.
- 11. 1st Lowland Brigade T.M.B.
- 12. 28th Field Ambulance.
- 13. Section 34th Field Coy. R.E.
- 14. "A" Battery 50th Bde. R.F.A.
- 15. "A" Coy. 9th M.G. Bn.
- 16. Composite Coy. 8th Cyclist Battn.
- 18. Lowland Division "G"
- 18. Lowland Division "Q"
- 19. 2nd Lowland Brigade.
- 20. 3rd Lowland Brigade.
- 21. 2nd Highland Brigade.
- 22. 63rd Bde. R.G.A.
- 23. 105th Coy. R.A.S.C.
- 24. & 25 War Diary.
- 26, 27 & 28. Spare.
- 29. File Copy
- 30. 1/6th K.O.S.B.

Appendix F.

Secret.

ADVANCE INTO GERMANY.

1st LOWLAND BRIGADE ORDER No 283

Reference Maps.

Germany 2K 1/100000
Germany 2S N.W. 1/25000

18th June 1919.

1. The Lowland Brigade Group will advance on 20th June and occupy ELBERFELD and the high ground on the general line A9595 - A8690 - A7800, A6080 - A5680 - A4575 and A3773.

2. The march of the Brigade Group will be covered by an advance guard composed of the following units and under the command of :-

   Lieut. Col. A.B. THORBURN 15th H.L.I.
   "A" Coy. 8th Cyclists Battn. (3 platoons)
   "A" Batty. 50th Bde. R.F.A.
   15th H.L.I.

3. (a) The advanced guard less 1 Platoon of cyclists and 1 Coy. of infantry will move by the KIUSE - VOHWINKEL - WIEDEN - SAARENHAUS - BERGERHEIDE - STEINBERG - BIRKEN - METZ MACHERAIM - LENGENFELD ROAD and will occupy an outpost position on the high ground mentioned in para 1.
   On the occupation of the outpost line by the Infantry being completed H.Q. and 1 Platoon of cyclists Coy. will be ordered up by O.C. Advanced guard to proceed to billeting area ELBERFELD.
   (b) One platoon of cyclists and 1 Coy. of infantry will move by the VOHWINKEL - SONBORN - ELBERFELD ROAD as far as the line LICHTENSCHIED - ELBERFELD ROAD in B14,15.05 and the hill B0534.
   When BARMEN has been occupied by troops of the Southern Division, the Cyclist Platoon will proceed to its billeting Area, and the infantry Company will rejoin its Battalion.
   Liaison Posts, strength of each one section, will be established by Outpost Commander at Road Junction B.0891 and A.3773.

4. The starting point for the main body will be the road junction 150 yards south of KIUSE POST, A.3612.
   The hour at which the head of the Column is to pass this point on 20th June will be known as ZERO HOUR and will be notified to the advanced guard Commander and Units of the main body by wire.

2.

5. The order of march, time of passing the starting point and route to be followed by main body is given in attached table.

6. The distances to be maintained between Battalions and between Companies of the main body on the march are 20 yards and 10 yards respectively.
20 yards will be maintained between Battalions and other Units.
The Column will halt at 10 minutes to each clock hour during the march, and will resume the march at the hour.

7. During the advance RED Very lights (1") will be used by the infantry to indicate that their advance is being resisted by the enemy.

8. The Brigade Report Centre will, in the first instance be at the head of the main guard and on arrival at ELBERFELD at the Main Telegraph Office, MORIAN STRASSE. The position of Brigade Headquarters will be notified to Units after arrival.
On completion of the march the location of Units of the Brigade Group will be as follows:-

1 Platoon of Cyclists
A. Battery 50th Brigade R.F.A. } On outpost with Headquarters at DORRENBURG.
15th H.L.I.

Brigade Headquarters.
1st Lowland Bde. L.T.M.B.
1 sect. 64th Field Coy. R.E.
A. Coy. 9th Bn. M.G. Corps
A. Coy. 8th Cyclists Bn less one platoon
28th Field Ambulance
105th Coy. R.A.S.C.
1/5th K.O.S.B.
} ELBERFELD.

All Units will report by orderly the exact location of their Headquarters immediately after occupation.

9. The following guards to be mounted in ELBERFELD will be detailed by 51st H.L.I.:-

MAIN TELEGRAPH OFFICE	1 platoon less 2 sections
GAS WORKS	1 section
ELECTRIC POWER ST. SIMONSTRASSE	1 section.
RAILWAY MANAGEMENT OFFICE	1 platoon less 2 sections
RAILWAY WORKSHOPS	2 sections
" ENGINE SHED	1 platoon less 2 sections
" STATION	2 sections.

The above guards will march with that part of the advanced guard referred to in para. 3 sub para. (b) and will take up their duties immediately on arrival in the Town.

3.

Notices will be given to these guards and these will be posted up by them near their posts and in and about the Railway buildings.

O.C. 51st H.L.I. will detail an officer to command the guards on the march, to see that they are mounted in the proper places and to give them orders.

In addition to the above guards, Battalions will mount guards on important Railway Bridges and tunnels in or near ELBERFELD. Separate information and instructions relating to the protection of the Railway system have been issued.

The special duty of all guards mounted in accordance with this paragraph will be to compel all German personnel to remain at their posts, more especially the head managers and sub managers, to stop all movements of trains until the Railways have been taken over by the SOUS-COMMISSION of the C.I.F.C.F.C. and to prevent damages to Bridges, Tunnels, permanent way, rolling stock, buildings and machinery.

10. The Brigade Headquarters Guard will march with the Headquarters and will be relieved at retreat on 20th and 21st June by a guard furnished by the 51st H.L.I.

11. Inlying piquets will be detailed as follows:- Each Battalion other than the Outpost Bn. 1 Company. Other Units, 25% of strength.
These piquets will be ready to turn out at a moments notice on the alarm being given.

12. Each Unit will have an alarm post which will be known to all ranks in the Unit.

13. Watches will be sychronized by the Brigade Signal Officer at Brigade Headquarters at 18.00 hours on 19th June. All Units are to send representatives.

14. All prisoners captured and all documents secured will be sent to Brigade Headquarters.

15. Brigade Headquarters will close at PIEPERSBURG at ZERO HOUR on 20th June.

Acknowledge.

W. Carter

Captain,
Brigade Major,
1st Lowland Brigade.

TABLE TO ACCOMPANY 1st LOWLAND BRIGADE ORDER No. 238 dated 17/3/19.

Order of March	Unit.	Time of Passing Starting Point.	Route.
1	Brigade Headquarters	ZERO	GRAFRATH, VOGNTIKEL - SCHMIDT - HEBER: FELD Road.
2	1st Lowland Bde. T.M.B.	ZERO + 1 min.	Do.
3	1 section 54th Field Coy. R.E.	ZERO + 1½ "	Do.
4	A. Coy. 9th Bn. H.C. Corps	ZERO + 2 "	Do.
5	5Lt H.L.I.	ZERO + 4 "	Do.
6	1/5th K.O.S.B.	ZERO + 12 "	Do.
7	23th Field Ambulance	ZERO + 20 "	Do.
8	105th Coy. R.A.S.C.	ZERO + 24 "	Do.

Appendix 9

ADVANCE INTO GERMANY.

1st LOWLAND BRIGADE INSTRUCTIONS No. 7.

19th June, 1919.

1. J. day will not be tomorrow, 20th June. The date will be notified later.

2. All units will be ready to carry out Brigade Order No. 288 dated 18th June, 1919, at short notice.

3. Move forecasted for J. + 1 day and subsequent days in 1st Lowland Brigade Instructions No. 2 dated 25th May, 1919, are dependent on the military situation on J. day.

4. When the advance commences the policy as regards the use of gas shell and long range artillery bombardment is - In principle these means will only be employed against positions or places which have definitely been ascertained to be occupied by a hostile force, which offering active resistance or by an insurgent population.

No gas shell will be used without Brigade sanction.

No H.E. bombardment without orders from B.H.Q.

Carter
Captain,
Brigade Major,
1st Lowland Brigade.

DISTRIBUTION.

Copies No.			
1	G.O.C.	8	1st Lowland Bde. L.T.M.B.
2	Brigade Major.	9	A. Coy. 9th M.G. Bn.
3	Staff Captain.	10	A. Battery 50th Brigade R.F.A.
4	Signal Officer.	11	A. Coy. 8th Cyclist Bn.
5	1/5th K.O.S.B.	12	105th Coy. R.A.S.C.
6	15th H.L.I.	13	28th Field Ambulance.
7	51st H.L.I.	14	Section 64th Field Coy. R.E.

Appendix H.

1st LOWLAND BRIGADE ORDER No. 293.

Reference Map
    SOLINGEN Sheet.   20th June, 1919.

1.   The 51st H.L.I. will move to the STOCKER, OBENSCHEIDT and DELLEIT AREA tomorrow, 21st June, 1919.

         Move to be completed by 12.00 hours.

2.   Billets will be alloted by Staff Captain, Civil Administration, No. 2 Sub-Area.

3.   Completion of move to be reported to Brigade Headquarters also location of new Battalion Headquarters.

Acknowledge.

                                             Captain,
                                         Brigade Major,
                                   1st Lowland Brigade.

Copy No. 1.   G.O.C.
          2.   Brigade Major.
          3.   Staff Captain.
          4.   Staff Captain, Civil Administration.
          5.   Signal Officer.
          6.   1/5th K.O.S.B.
          7.   15th H.L.I.
          8.   51st H.L.I.
         10.   1st Lowland Bde. L.T.M.B.
         10.   A. Coy. 9th M.G. Battn.
         11.   A. Battery 50th Bde. R.F.A.
         12.   A. Coy. 8th Cyclist Battn.
         13.   105th Coy. R.A.S.C.
         14.   28th Field Ambulance.
         15.   Section 64th Field Coy. R.E.
   16 & 17. War Diary.
         18.   File.

Appendix 2

ADVANCE INTO GERMANY.

AMENDMENT to 1st LOWLAND BRIGADE INSTRUCTIONS No 2.

AMENDMENT No 5.

Para 20   J day Line 1 delete the words VOHWINKEL &
Para 21
Delete
105th Coy. R.A.S.C. (Refilling Point) 2 N.C.O's and 6 Men.

Para 5 for "C" Battery read "A" Battery.
Para 20 J - 1 day for "C" Battery read "A" Battery.

W. Carter
Captain.
Brigade Major,
1st Lowland Brigade.

SECRET

ADVANCE INTO GERMANY

20/6/19

The following Amendments will be made to 1st LOWLAND BRIGADE INSTRUCTIONS NO 2 dated 25/5/19.

(a) Para 12 as amended on 27/5/19 delete the figure and words " 1 Horse Ambulance" in line 11.
In line 12 delete the words " each Battalion" and substitute " the Advanced Guard".
In line 13 delete the words "those to Units" and substitute "this vehicle to report to O.C. Advanced Guard" on the night before the Advance.

W. Carter
Captain,
Brigade Major,
1st Lowland Brigade.

Appendix J

SECRET.

ADVANCE INTO GERMANY

20/6/19.

The following Amendments will be made to 1st LOWLAND BRIGADE ORDER No 288 dated 18th June 1919.

(a) Para 4 delete the words " the road Junction 150 yards south of" and substitute "cross roads at"

(b) Para 8 after 1st Lowland Brigade T.M.B. add "51st H.L.I."

Martin

Captain,
Brigade Major,
1st Lowland Brigade.

DISTRIBUTION.

Copy No 1. G.O.C.
2. Brigade Major.
3. Staff Captain.
4. Staff Captain (Civil Administration.)
5. Signal Officer.
6. Orderly Officer.
7. Provost Officer.
8. 1/5th K.O.S.B.
9. 15th H.L.I.
10. 51st H.L.I.
11. 1st Lowland Bde. T.M.B.
12. 28th Field Ambulance.
13. 105th Coy. R.A.S.C.
14. 64th R.Es.
15. 50th Bde. R.F.A. (for Q Battery.)
16. 9th Bn. M.G.Bn. Corps. (for A Coy.)
17. Composite Cyclist Coy.
18. Lowland Division 'G'
19. Lowland Division 'Q'
20. 2nd Lowland Brigade.
21. 3rd Lowland Brigade.
22. 2nd Highland Brigade.
23. Southern Division for X Brigade.
24. Southern Division for Y Brigade.
25. 19th H.L.I.
26. 63rd Bde. R.G.A.
27. Tank Battalion.
28. File Copy.
29 & 30. Wsr Diary.
31, 32, 33 Spare.

ADVANCE INTO GERMANY.

SECRET

1st LOWLAND BRIGADE ORDER No 294.

23/6/19.

Reference Maps.
Germany 2 K 1/100,000
" 2 S.N.W. 1/25,000.

1. All preparation will be made to commence moves laid down in 1st Lowland Brigade Order No 288 dated 18th June at 03.15 hours on 24th June.

2. The points of the advanced Guard will be at KLUSE POST ready to cross the perimeter at the above mentioned hour but they will not move forward until Orders are issued by a Staff Officer at KLUSE POST to do so.

3. The leading Units of the main body 1st Lowland Brigade Group will be prepared to pass the Starting Point at 03.45 hours (Zero hour.) and the remaining Units at the times stated in the table sent out with order No 288.
Should the Advance not commence at 03.15 hours Brigade Headquarters will not move on to the starting point until the advanced Guard is clear.

4. The Guards referred to in Para 9 of Brigade Order No 288 will move to Piepersberg tonight arriving there not later than 23 hours. They will be at KLUSE POST CROSS Roads at 03.15 hours tomorrow and the O.C. will report to O.C. advanced Guard at that time.

5. From 16.00 hours today an Officer must be in the Office of each Unit.

6. Contact Aeroplanes of the 7th Squadron R.A.F. will fly a yellow and red streamer from their tails and will also carry black flaps attached to the rear edge of the lower plane, one on each side of the body.

Lorries will report to units at a late hour to-night.

Acknowledge.

DISTRIBUTION.

Copy No.	1.	G.O.C.
	2.	Brigade Major
	3.	Staff Captain
	4.	Staff Captain (Civil Administration)
	5.	Signal Officer
	6.	Orderly Officer
	7.	Provost Officer
	8.	1/5th K.O.S.B.
	9.	15th H.L.I.
	10.	51st H.L.I.
	11.	1st Lowland Brigade T.M.B.
	12.	28th Field Ambulance
	13.	Section 64th Field Coy R.E.
	14.	"A" Battery 50th Bde. R.F.A.
	15.	"A" Coy. 9th M.G.Bn.
	16.	Composite Coy. 8th Cyclist Battn.
	17.	Lowland Division "G"
	18.	Lowland Division "Q"
	19.	2nd Lowland Brigade.
	20.	3rd Lowland Brigade.
	21.	2nd Highland Brigade.
	22.	63rd Bde. R.G.A.
	23.	105th Coy. R.A.S.C.
	24. & 25	War Diary.
	26, 27 & 28	Spare.
	29.	File Copy.

MESSAGE FORM. Series No. of Message _____

	Recd.		
In CALL v___	At___ Sent	By___	Army Form C 2128 (pads of 100)
Out___ v___	At___	By___	

PREAMBLE _____

M.M. Offices { Delivery _____ v
{ Origin _____

Date Stamp *appended* ✓

PREFIX **PRIORITY**   Words _____

TO:
1/5th K.O.S.B.   105th Coy. R.A.S.C.
15th H.L.I.   28th Field Ambulance
51st H.L.I.   64th Field Coy. R.E.
1st Lowland Bde. T.M.B.

FROM & Place: _____

Originator's Number	Day of Month	In reply to Number
S.C. 96	23	

Official wire received that Boche will sign tonight as No move takes place tomorrow.

(Sgd) Capt.,
Staff Capt.

TIME OF ORIGIN _____   TIME OF HANDING IN (For Signal use only) _____

Originator's Signature (Not Telegraphed) _____

MESSAGE FORM.

PREFIX **PRIORITY**

TO 'A' Bty. 50th Bde. R.F.A.
    'A' Coy. 9th Bn. M.G.C.
    'A' Coy. 8th Composite Cyclist Bn.

FROM & Place: 1st Lowland Brigade.

Originator's Number: S.G. 96
Day of Month: 23

Official wire received that Boche will sign tonight as No move takes place tomorrow.

(Sgd) Capt.,
Staff Capt.

ADVANCE INTO GERMANY.

SECRET.

1st LOWLAND BRIGADE INSTRUCTIONS NO 8.

Ref. Map.
Tracing attached.

1. On arrival in ELBERFELD Units of the Brigade Group will be billeted in the area shown on attached tracing.

2. Immediately the Billeting Area is reached each Unit will at once arrange for the defence of their Area.

3. Machine Gun, Lewis Gun and Rifle Posts will be established at cross roads, Open Spaces and on Verandahs and roofs of houses etc.
The inlying picquets refered to in para 11 of 1st Lowland Brigade Order No. 208 dated 18th June 1919 will not be utilised for this purpose as they must remain intact and ready to turn out at a moments notice.

4. As great a display of force as possible will be shown in order to impress upon the inhabitants the fact that the town is in occupation of BRITISH TROOPS.

5. If the town is quiet and after the defence arrangements have been completed, and the billeting has been done, posts not required to remain in position will be withdrawn to their Alarm Posts and from there to their billets.

6. The withdrawal from posts to Billets is not to be done hurriedly and certainly not before dinners are ready for the men.

7. Headquarters of Units, except 1st Lowland Brigade T. M. B. will be established along the KONIGSTRASSE, KAISERSTRASSE and BERLINER::STRASSE.

W. Carlin
Captain,
Brigade Major,
1st Lowland Brigade.

DISTRIBUTION.

Copy No. 1.   G.O.C.
    2.   Brigade Major.
    3.   Staff Captain.
    4.   Staff Captain (Civil Administration)
    5.   Signal Officer.
    6.   Orderly Officer.
    7.   Provost Officer.
*8.   1/5th. K.O.S.B.
*9.   15th. H.L.I.
*10.   51st. H.L.I.
*11.   1st Lowland Brigade T.M.B.
*12.   28th. Field Ambulance.
*13.   Section 64th. Field Coy. R.E.
  14.   "A" Battery 50th. Bde. R.F.A.
*15.   "A" Coy. 9th. M.G. Bn.
*16.   Composite Coy. 8th. Cyclist Battn.
  17.   Lowland Division G.
  18.   Lowland Division Q.
  19.   2nd. Lowland Brigade.
*20.   105th Coy R.A.S.C.
21.& 22. War Diary.
23, 24 &25 spare.
26.   File Copy.

SECRET

Appendix N

1st LOWLAND BRIGADE ORDER No 296

26.6.19.

Reference Map.
Sheet Solingen.

1. The 1st Lowland Brigade Group (less 51st H.L.I. and "A" Coy 8th Cyclist Battalion.) will move to the SOLINGEN AREA on A & C days in accordance with attached march table.
   "A" day will be notified to Units later.

2. Units will move independently and on completion of March will occupy accommodation vacated by them on 19th inst.

3. The Civil Administration of No 1 Sub-Area will be taken over from 2nd Highland Brigade by Noon on "C" day.

4. Lorries will report to Unit Headquarters at 07.30 hours on the day Units move. These lorries will be sent back to their park in the evening of the same day.

5. Completion of March to be reported by wire to Brigade Headquarters.

6. Brigade Headquarters will close at PIEPERSBERG at 14.00 hours on C day and will re-open at SOLINGEN at the same time.

7. 5 Tents held on charge of A Battery 50th Bde R.F.A. will be handed in to D.A.D.O.S. Lowland Division at OHLIGS on D day.

Captain,
Brigade Major,
1st Lowland Brigade.

DISTRIBUTION.

Copy No				
1	G.O.C.	13	Lowland Division "Q"
2	Brigade Major.	14	2nd Highland Bde.
3	Staff Captain.	15	2nd Lowland Bde.
4	Bde. Signal Officer.	16	105th Coy. R.A.S.C.
5	Provost Officer.	17 & 18	War Diary.
6	1/5th K.O.S.B.	19	File
7	15th H.L.I.	20	Staff Captain (Civil Administration.)
8	51st H.L.I.		
9	1st Lowland Bde. T.M.B.	21	"A" Coy. 9th M.G.C.
10	28th Field Ambulance.	22	"A" Bty. 50th Bde R.F.A.
11	64th Field Coy. R.E.	23	Orderly Officer.
12	Lowland Division "G"		

MARCH TABLE ISSUED WITH 1st LOWLAND BRIGADE ORDER No. 296 dated 28th June, 1919.

Day.	Unit.	Starting Point	Hour of Passing	Route	Destination	Remarks.
A. day	A. Coy. 5th K.O.S.B.	Coy. H.Q.	—	No restriction.	LANGENFELD	LANGENFELD Dump guard to be taken over before 12 noon.
C. day	105th Coy. R.A.S.C.	Cross Roads F.4179.	14.00 hours	CENTRAL-SOLINGEN-HOHSCHIED Road	SOLINGEN	
"	1/5th K.O.S.R.	Do.	14.10 hours	Do.	Do.	
"	38th Field Ambulance	Do.	14.30 hours	CENTRAL-SOLINGEN-OHLIGS Road	Do.	
"	1st Lowland Bde. T.M.B.	Do.	14.40 hours	CENTRAL-SOLINGEN Road	Do.	
"	A. Battery 50th Bde. F.A.	Do.	14.50 hours	CENTRAL-SOLINGEN-HOHSCHIED Road	HOHSCHIED.	
"	15th H.L.I.	Do.	15.10 hours	CENTRAL-SOLINGEN Road	SOLINGEN.	
"	1st Lowland Bde. H.Q.	Do.	15.30 hours	Do.	Do.	
"	Section 34th Field Coy. R.E.	Do.	15.40 hour	Do.	Do.	

SECRET

War Diary

1st LOWLAND BRIGADE ORDER No 295

Reference Map.
SOLINGEN.

26.6.19.

1. The 51st H.L.I. will relieve 51st Bn Gordon Highland--ers in the line before 12.00 hours on "C" day. "C" day will be notified later.
    Headquarters and Company in reserve will take over and occupy the accommodation in SOLINGEN previously allotted to the Unit.

2. The details of relief will be arranged between Battalion Commanders direct.

3. All Order Boards, Instructions and Copy of Defence Scheme previously handed over to 51st Gordon Highlanders will be taken over on relief.
    Stores held on charge at the Outposts will be taken over and receipt given to outgoing Unit.

4. All Officers, N.C.Os and Men will be warned that they are not to fire on civilians under any cirsumstances. Order Boards will be amended accordingly.

5. Lorries will report at Battalion Headquarters on morning of relief. These lorries will be sent back to the Park by the evening of the day on which the relief takes place.

6. 15 Tents at present in charge of Units will be handed in to DADOS Lowland Division at OHLIGS on "D" day.

Captain,
Brigade Major,
1st Lowland Brigade.

DISTRIBUTION.

Copy No		Copy No	
1	G.O.C.	11	64th Field Coy R.E.
2	Brigade Major.	12	Lowland Division "G"
3	Staff Captain.	13	Lowland Division "Q"
4	Bde. Signal Officer.	14	2nd Highland Brigade
5	Provost Officer.	15	2nd Lowland Brigade
6	1/5th K.O.S.B.	16	105th Coy R.A.S.C.
7	15th H.L.I.	17&18	War Diary
8	51st H.L.I.	19	File
9	1st Lowland Bde. T.M.B.	20	Staff Captain (Civil Administration.)
10	28th Field Ambulance.		

MESSAGE FORM. Series No. of Message _____

In CALL	v	Recd. At	By	Army Form C 2128.
Out	v	Sent At	By	(pads of 100)

PREAMBLE

Date Stamp

M.M. Offices — Delivery _____ v
Origin _____

PREFIX PRIORITY   Words

TO:
"A" Bty 50th Bde R.F.A.
1/5th K.O.S.B.   165th Coy. R.A.S.C.
15th H.L.I.   28th Field Ambulance
51st H.L.I.   1st Lowland T.M.B.
"A" Coy 9th Bn M.G.C.

Originator's Number	Day of Month	In reply to Number
B.M./1b/778	28	

Peace	is	signed aaa	Reference
Brigade	Orders	295	and
296	"A" DAY	will	be
30th June	"C" DAY	2nd July aaa	
Acknowledge			

TIME OF ORIGIN

TIME OF HANDING IN (For Signal use only)

(Sgd) Capt
Brigade Major.

Originator's Signature (Not Telegraphed)

WAR DIARY
or
INTELLIGENCE SUMMARY.

(Erase heading not required.)

Army Form C. 2118.

15th H.L.I.
1st Gaz Bde
1st Horse [?] [?]

Place	Date	Hour	Summary of Events and Information	Remarks and references to Appendices
[illegible]	[?]	1 p.	Very warm. Church parade as usual	T&P
	2nd		Warm. Inspection of Battalion by Capt. [?] Plans Army.	T&P
	3rd		Warm. King's birthday parade. Battalion engaging their Royal Salute guns. — Remainder of day known as holiday.	T&P
	4th		Full Dress turning outs by companies. Lecture in the Konocurs by Regt. in afternoon. "A" & "B" on The Past Present and Future of British Americans Three-ship. Other Coys — nothing of coy. a	T&P
	5th		Warm. Listen. Wining uniforms from "a" to "B" [?] of his association with Batt. [?]	T&P
	6th		11 a.m. It was raining. Orders [?] in afternoon. 15th H.L.I & 1st K.O.S.B. 15 [?] for the 15th H.L.I.	T&P
	7th	10. a.	C.O.s inspection of Billets.	T&P
	8th		Showery. School Parade as usual. Picking up [?] community	T&P
	9th		Showery [?] [?] guides [?] [?] arrangements	T&P
	10th		[?] [?] [?] [?] [?] [?] arrangement	T&C
	11th		Warm [?] [?] [?] [?] [?] [?]	T&P

430
3 sheets

28031 W3125/M2250 1000m 6/17 M.R.Co.,Ltd. (1367) Forms W3091.   Army Form W. 3091.

Cover for Documents.

Leave Return
Natures of Enclosures.

Notes, or Letters written.

1st Lowland Brigade Headquarters.

July, 1919.

Army Form C. 2118.

CONFIDENTIAL

WAR DIARY

INTELLIGENCE SUMMARY.

(Erase heading not required.)

Instructions regarding War Diaries and Intelligence Summaries are contained in F. S. Regs., Part II. and the Staff Manual respectively. Title pages will be prepared in manuscript.

Place	Date	Hour	Summary of Events and Information	Remarks and references to Appendices
PIEPERSBERG	July 1st		Showery. Brigade prepares to move back to original billets at SOLINGEN. Orders were issued during last week in June and forwarded under June Diary.	
SOLINGEN	" 2nd		Very showery. Brigade moves back to SOLINGEN. 51st H.L.I. take over outpost line from 51st Gordons.	
"	" 3rd		Dull and prospects of rain. Training was carried out under Battalion arrangements.	
"	" 4th		Observed as a holiday.	
"	" 5th		Weather improves. Lt.-Col. F.S. THACKERAY, D.S.O., assumed command of 15th H.L.I. and Major A.B. THORBURN took over duties of Second in Command.	
"	" 6th		Weather good but dull. Church Parades as per Brigade Routine Orders. A special United Thanksgiving Service was held. Major D.M. MURRAY LYON, D.S.O., M.C., joined 51st H.L.I.	
"	" 7th		Training under Battalion arrangements. 15th H.L.I. played 51st Hants at cricket. Result - 15th H.L.I. = 38, 51st Hants = 30.	
"	" 8th		Training under Battalion arrangements. "C" Coy., 15th H.L.I., were firing on Stockerberger Range. 1st Lowland Brigade Instructions No. 1 were issued to Units re move to take over 1st Light Brigade Area. Appendix "A".	
"	" 9th		Training under Battalion arrangements. 1st Lowland Brigade Orders with March Table issued on Appendix "B".	
"	" 10th		Advance party of 13th K.R.R.C. take over O.H.Q.GS Railhead Guard. Battalions prepare to move to new Area.	
"	" 11th		Very heavy rain. Brigade moves to new area in accordance with orders previously issued. See Appendices M & B
DORMAGEN	" 12th		Battalions clean billets and billet inspections by C.O.s. Lt. Col. F.S. THACKERAY proceeded to join 2nd Battalion H.L.I. at ALDERSHOT. Major A.B. THORBURN re-assumes command.	
"	" 13th		Showery. Church Parades as per Brigade Routine Orders.	

CONFIDENTIAL
WAR DIARY
or
INTELLIGENCE SUMMARY

(Erase heading not required.)

Army Form C. 2118.

Place	Date	Hour	Summary of Events and Information	Remarks and references to Appendices
DORMAGEN	July 14th		Dull but mild. Training under Battalion arrangements.	
	15th		Mild. Training under Battalion arrangements. Inter-Company Cricket Match in 15th H.L.I.	
	16th		Warm. Training under Battalion arrangements. 15th H.L.I. played 51st H.L.I. at cricket. Win for 15th H.L.I.	
	17th		Very Warm. Training under Battalion arrangements.	
	18th		Mild. Training under Battalion arrangements.	
	19th		Warm. Baths under Battalion arrangements. 1/5th K.O.S.B. held Sports Meeting. Holiday. "C" Company, 15th H.L.I., hold sports. 51st H.L.I. hold examination on Army School Certificates.	
	20th		Showery. Church Parades as per Brigade Routine Orders. Officers v. Men of 15th H.L.I.. Win for N.C.O.s and men. 1st Lowland Brigade Order No. 298 issued re move of Brigade Headquarters to Hs ARFF. Appendix "C".	
	21st		Very wet. Training under Battalion arrangements.	
	22nd		Wet. Training under Battalion arrangements.	
	23rd		Showery. Training under Battalion arrangements. 15th H.L.I. held Inter-Company Cross Country Run. Lecture by Major WADE. Brigade Headquarters moved to Hs. ARFF in accordance with 1st Lowland Brigade Order 298. Appendix "C".	
	24th		Showery. Training under Battalion arrangements.	
	25th		Dull. Training under Battalion arrangements. 15th H.L.I. held a dance in their Dining Hall.	
	26th		15th H.L.I. held Battalion Sports. Other Units training as per programme.	
Hs ARFF	27th		Dull. Church Parades as per Brigade Routine Orders. 15th H.L.I. plays Divisional Headquarters at cricket. Win for 15th H.L.I.	

CONFIDENTIAL

WAR DIARY
~~INTELLIGENCE SUMMARY~~

(Erase heading not required.)

Army Form C. 2118.

Instructions regarding War Diaries and Intelligence Summaries are contained in F.S. Regs., Part II. and the Staff Manual respectively. Title pages will be prepared in manuscript.

Place	Date	Hour	Summary of Events and Information	Remarks and references to Appendices
Hs ARFF	July 28th		Dull. 51st H.L.I. held Battalion Sports. Other Units training as per programme.	
"	29th		Very Wet. Training under Battalion arrangements.	
"	30th		Dull. Training under Battalion arrangements. 15th H.L.I. played 1/5th K.O.S.B. at football. Win for 15th H.L.I.	
"	31st		Dull. Training under Battalion arrangements. Lecture by Rev. C.H. HEASETT, B.A., on Venereal Disease.	

Hugh Copp
Pat Major
for Brigadier-General,
Commanding 1st Lowland Brigade.

Appendix "A" War Diary

DISTRIBUTION.

No 1 Copy.	G.O.C.
2	Brigade Major.
3	Staff Captain.
4	Staff Captain (Civil Administration.)
5	Signal Officer.
6	Provost Officer.
7	Orderly Officer.
8	1/5th K.O.S.B.
9	15th H.L.I.
10	51st H.L.I.
11	1st Lowland Bde. T.M.B.
12	28th Field Ambulance.
13	105th Coy. R.A.S.J.
14	64th Field Coy. R.E.
15	Lowland Division "G"
16	Lowland Division "Q"
17	1st Light Brigade.
18	R.T.O. Opladen.
19	2nd Lowland Brigade.
20	3rd Lowland Brigade.
21,22, & 23	File and Spare.
24 & 25	War Diary.

MOVE TO DORMAGEN AREA.

1st LOWLAND BRIGADE INSTRUCTIONS No 1.

Reference Maps.

1 K 1/100,000
2 K 1/100,000

8th July 1919.

1. RELIEF.

The 1st Lowland Brigade Group will relieve the 1st Light Brigade in the Dormagen Area on 11th July 1919.

2. MOVE.

Moves of both Personnel and Transport will be by rail, lorry and road in accordance with attached tables.

3. CIVIL ADMINISTRATION AND PROVOST OFFICE STAFF

The Civil Administration and Provost Office Staff as detailed below will remain at SOLINGEN.

(a) Civil Administration.　　(b) Provost Staff.

Capt. F. Reeves, M.C.,　　　　Lieut. A. Ellis M.A.C.
　Staff Captain Civil　　　　　No 29329 Pte T. Dutters
　　Administration.　　　　　　　1/5th K.O.S.P.
280345
　Sgt. E. Abrahams 15th H.L.I.
74247 Pte A. Morrison
　51st H.L.I.　　Batman.
57133 Pte J. Colquhoun
　15th H.L.I.　　Groom.

4. ADVANCED PARTIES /

4. ADVANCED PARTIES.

(a) Advanced Parties, strength as under, will move to 1st Light Brigade Area on 10th inst. for the purpose of taking over billeting accommodation etc, and for guiding Units to their billeting areas on arrival at DORMAGEN STATION.

UNIT	OFFICERS	O.R.s
Brigade Headquarters	1	4
1/5th K.O.S.B.	1	5
15th H.L.I.	1	5
51st H.L.I.	1	5
1st Lowland Bde. T.M.B.	1	1
105 Coy. R.A.S.C.	1	1
64th Field Coy. R.Es.	2x	2x
28th Field Ambulance	1	1
	9	24

x 1 to take over work shops and work at DORMAGEN.

The above will report at Brigade Headquarters at 09.30 hours on 10th inst. where lorries will be in readiness to convey them to new area. The senior officer will command the party.

The unconsumed portion of the day's rations and rations for 11th inst. will be taken. Kits and blankets will be taken.

(b) Advanced Parties, strength similar to those furnished by this Brigade Group will arrive in 1st Lowland Brigade Area from 1st Light Brigade on 10th inst.

They will be accommodated by Units whom they are relieving.

They will bring rations with them.

5. RELIEF of 51st H.L.I.

The relief of 51st H.L.I. in the line will be carried out by two Companies 18th K.R.R.C. on the evening of 10th inst.

The Companies 18th K.R.R.C. will arrive by lorries at Brigade Headquarters at 19.00 hours where a guide will conduct them to 51st H.L.I. Billets at FREDERICK STRASSE.

51st H.L.I. will provide the Companies with tea on arrival and afterwards they will be conveyed in the lorries to the Headquarters of the Companies in the line.

Relief will then be carried out and the Companies relieved will be conveyed back to SOLINGEN by the lorries.

1 Officer per Company and 1 N.C.O. per Post will remain in the line with the new Unit until 06.00 hours on 11th inst. when they will rejoin their Headquarters.

Copy of Brigade and Unit's Defence Scheme, Order Boards and any Instructions with reference to Perimeter Posts issued, will be handed over on relief.

Completion of relief will be wired to Brigade Headquarters.

(3)

6   GUARDS

    (a)   The 15th H.L.I. will furnish a Guard, strength
          2 Officers, 2 Sergeants, 4 Corporals, 1 Bugler
          and 47 Other Ranks, on the DORMAGEN Factory,
          relieving a similar guard now furnished by 13th
          K.R.R.C.
          This Guard will be formed from two complete
          Platoons if possible.
          It will proceed by the 13.12 hours train from
          SOLINGEN STATION on 10th inst. changing at COLOGNE
          for DORMAGEN, and proceeding by the train for that
          Station arriving at 17.44 hours.

    (b)   1/5th K.O.S.B. will furnish a Guard of one
          Section of not less than 1 N.C.O. and 6 Men from
          the Company to be quartered at STRUZELBERG, for the
          ST. PETERS CROSS ROADS POST, relieving a guard of
          20th K.R.R.C.
          The train arrangements for this Guard will be
          the same as for (a)
          Rations for 10th and 11th will be taken by both
          Guards, also 1 Blanket per man and Officers' kits.
          The 1st Light Brigade are being asked to provide
          transport to convey Officers' baggage from the
          Station to DORMAGEN.

    (c)   The permanent Guard at the STADTHAUS DETENTION
          ROOMS will be relieved by a Guard to be furnished
          by the Traffic Control Squadron at Retreat on 10th
          inst.

    (d)   Brigade Headquarters guard will march off at
          12.00 hours on 11th inst. and will proceed to the
          new Area by the last troop train, due to leave
          SOLINGEN STATION at 13.00 hours. On arrival at
          DORMAGEN the guard will mount at Brigade Headquarters
          and will be relieved at Retreat in the usual way.

    (e)   The OHLIGS RAILHEAD GUARD will be relieved by
          a guard of 1st Light Brigade during the afternoon
          of 10th inst. On relief the relieved Guard will
          rejoin its Unit at SOLINGEN.

    (f)   The Guard on 104th Coy R.A.S.C. Ration Dump,
          OHLIGS, will not mount on 10th inst. as 104th Coy
          R.A.S.C. move on that date.

          All boards of orders, Guard Room utensils, etc.
          will be handed over on relief.

7 LORRIES

Lorries will be provided as laid down in Table below. All stores which cannot be carried on these lorries or on the Horse Transport will be conveyed by rail.

Date	Time	No of Lorries	Reporting at	Load	Remarks.
July 10th	10.00 hours.	2	Bde. Hqrs.	Advance Party to DORMAGEN	Return to BEDBURG on completion
10th	18.00 hours	1	28th Field Ambulance.	Stores to Stn. only.	Report to Bde H.Q. on completion
10th	18.30 hours	2	1/5th K.O.S.B.	Stores	
10th	18.30 hours	2	15th H.L.I.	Stores	
10th	18.30 hours	2	51st H.L.I.	Stores	
10th	18.30 hours	1	105th Coy R.A.S.C. L.T.M.B.	Stores.	½ share to each Unit.
10th	18.30 hours	1	64th Coy R.E.	Stores	

These lorries except two for Advance Parties will be used to carry stores which are being sent by rail to SOLINGEN Railway Station in the early morning of 11th inst., after which they will return to the Unit Headquarters, reload and rendezvous at Brigade Headquarters not later than 10.00 hours.

The minimum number of personnel for loading and unloading the stores will travel on the lorries.

The senior N.C.O. or man riding on each lorry will have written instructions as to where the stores are to be off loaded.

Lorries will not be overloaded. No replacements are available in the event of a breakdown.

All lorries will travel in a convoy and not singly.

They will only do one journey from SOLINGEN to DORMAGEN AREA.

The 51st H.L.I. will detail an officer to take charge of the lorry convoy when it rendezvous at Brigade Headquarters. On completion of the journey to DORMAGEN AREA and after off loading, all lorries will rendezvous at Brigade Headquarters, DORMAGEN and from there will proceed to their park at Bedburg.

In addition to above, one lorry will meet each personnel train at DORMAGEN STATION to convey cooking utensils and rations carried on the troop train, to the destinations of Units.

Other lorries will meet baggage trains at ROMMERSKIRCHEN to convey the baggage not loaded on Horse Transport, to the Units to which it belongs.

(5)

8. ENTRAINING AND EMBARKATION STATES.

(a) All Units will render Entraining States to Brigade Headquarters by 14.00 hours, 10th July, in the following form.
All baggage and supply wagons, their drivers and their animals will be shown on Units' Entraining States.

Officers	Animals		Vehicles	
	O.R. / R.D.	All other animals	4 wheeled	2 wheeled

(b) A State similar to above will be rendered for all personnel, animals and vehicles proceeding by ferry.

9. DUTIES.

The following officers will supervise the entraining, embarking, detraining and disembarking of the Brigade Group.

(a) At SCHMIGEN — The Staff Captain, 1st Lowland Brigade, assisted by Capt. McNAUGHTON.

(b) At DORMAGEN — Lt. CAVE, Bde. Musketry Officer.

(c) At RODENKIRCHEN — An officer to be detailed by 15th H.L.I.

(d) At RHINE FERRY, BAYRATH — An officer to be detailed by 1/5th K.O.S.B.

(e) At RHINE FERRY, STURZELBERG — An officer to be detailed by 1/5th K.O.S.B.

With reference (b) and (c), the officers detailed will proceed by the first train to these stations.
Reference (d), the officer detailed will go to BAYRATH on 9th July to see the embarking of 2nd Brigade Transport at 10.00 hours, in order that he may see how the work is carried out. On the date of the move he will proceed to BAYRATH, reporting to the officer in charge of embarkation arrangements by 10.00 hours.
The officer detailed for duty at STURZELBERG will proceed across the Rhine on the first barge conveying Brigade Transport.

10. RETENTION ROOMS.

All soldiers in arrest confined in the STADTHAUS will be removed by the Unit to which the men belong by Retreat on 10th inst.; after which time no further admission of men belonging to 1st Lowland Brigade will be made.

11. INSTITUTE EMPLOY.

The Troops employed at the Y.M.C.A., Salvation Army Canteen and SCOTTISH CHURCHES HUT will rejoin their Units after the Institute where they are employed closes on 10th inst. 1st Light Brigade are being asked to send other men in their place.

12. DOCUMENTS, etc., TO BE HANDED OVER.

Maps vide B.M./2(a)/707 of 6/7/19, copies of Defence Scheme, details regarding Training and Recreation facilities of the present Area will be handed over to and those for the new Area will be taken over from Units being relieved.

Units will also obtain at the same time copies of orders regarding Bathing now in force in the DORTAGEN AREA. These orders will remain in force pending the issue of Brigade Instructions on the subject.

Before any bathing is permitted Units will ensure that these orders are known and understood by all ranks. In the past several cases of drowning have occurred through men disregarding these orders.

13. AMMUNITION, etc.

All mobile reserves of S.A.A., Grenades and Trench Mortar Ammunition will be handed over to the Advance Parties of 1st Light Brigade and receipts in duplicate obtained, one copy of which will be forwarded to Brigade Headquarters. Similarly our Advance Parties will take over in the new Area from Units they relieve, the mobile reserve of S.A.A., Grenades and Trench Mortar Ammunition held by those Units, and will give to those Units a receipt for Ammunition, etc., taken over and send a copy of the receipt to Brigade Headquarters.

14. SURPLUS BRIGADE EMPLOY.

All N.C.O's and men employed at Brigade Headquarters who are not required in the new Area will be returned to duty at Retreat on 10th inst. Names of men being returned will be notified to Units as early as possible.

15. **SUPPLIES.**

Supply Railhead will remain at OHLIGS up to and including Thursday, 10th July. From 11th inst. Railhead will be at BEDBURG.

Troops moving by train will entrain with the current days rations on the man or on the troop train. Rations for 12th inst. will be carried on the supply wagon which will move with Units. Rations for 13th inst. and afterwards will be delivered by lorry in the Area.

Transport moving by road will carry forage and rations for consumption on 11th inst.

16. **BILLETS.**

Billets will be handed over in a clean condition.

Units will hand over all requisitioned articles to the Unit relieving them. Receipts for all such articles handed over will be obtained in duplicate. One copy will be forwarded to Brigade Headquarters.

17. **ORDNANCE STORES.**

The Offices and Stores of D.A.D.O.S. are closed for the move. They will be reopened at LIPP on 11th inst.

18. **CLEAN CLOTHING STORES.**

The Clean Clothing Stores will be opened by the Baths Officer at BEDBURG on 11th inst.

19. **TENTAGE.**

Receipts in duplicate will be given and taken for all tentage handed over or taken over by Units. A copy of such receipts will be forwarded to Brigade Headquarters on completion of the move.

20. **HANDING OVER OF COMMAND.**

The Brigadier-General Commanding 1st Lowland Brigade will hand over the command of the Troops in, and the administration of No. 1 Sub-Area to the Lieut. Colonel Commanding 1st Light Brigade at 12.00 hours, 11th July, 1919.

21. LOCATION.

On arrival in the DORMAGEN AREA Units will be quartered as under:-

Unit.	Place.	Relieving.
(a) Brigade Headquarters	DORMAGEN	1st Light Bde H.Q.
(b) 15th H.L.I.	Do.	13th K.R.R.C.
(c) 51st H.L.I. H.Qrs.) 2 companies)	WORRINGEN	
1 company in camp near FUHLINGEN		
1 company	FUHLINGEN	18th K.R.R.C.
(d) 1/5th K.O.S.B. H.Qrs.) 3 companies)	ZONS	20th K.R.R.C.
1 company	STURZLEBERG	
(e) 64th Field Coy. R.E.	HORREN	226th Field Coy R.E.
(f) 28th Field Ambulance	SINNERSDORF	5th Field Ambnce.
(g) 105th Coy. R.A.S.C.	STRABERG	No. 3 Coy. Light Divisional Train.
(h) 1st Lowland Bde. L.T.M.B.	HACKENBCRICH	1st Light T.M.B.

22. BRIGADE HEADQUARTERS.

Brigade Headquarters will close at SOLINGEN at 12.00 hours on 11th inst., and will reopen at DORMAGEN at 16.00 hours on same date.

Captain,
Brigade Major,
1st Lowland Brigade.

TABLE "A".

ENTRAINMENT TABLE.

Unit.	No. of Train.	Nos. of Compts. and Covers for Personnel and Stats.	Time Units are due at SOLINGEN Station.	Time Train due to leave.	Station of arrival and Time due.	Nos. of Covers for Baggage on No. 3 TRAIN.	Remarks
Brigade H.Q.	No. 1	2 compartments for officers 6 covers	07.20 hrs.	08.54 hrs.	DORMAGEN 11.54 hrs.	3	All surplus baggage for Units travelling on No. 1 Train moves with its loading parties on No. 3 Train to ROMMERSKIRCHEN.
1st L.T.M.B.	No. 1	1 compartment 1 cover	07.20 "	"	"	1	
1/5th K.O.S.B.	No. 1	4 compartments 18 covers	07.25 "	"	"	5	
51st H.L.I.	No. 1	5 compartments 24 covers	07.40 "	"	"	5	
15th H.L.I.	No. 2	4 compartments 25 covers	07.55 "	09.08 "	DORMAGEN 12.17 hrs.	TRAIN No. 4. 5	All surplus baggage for Units travelling on No. 2 Train moves with its loading party on No. 4 Train to ROMMERSKIRCHEN.
94 Fd. Coy. R.E.	No. 2	1 compartment 5 covers	08.05 "	"	"	4	
28th Fd. Amb.	No. 2	1 compartment 3 covers	08.15 "	"	"	3	
105th Coy. RASC	No. 2	1 compartment	08.15 "	"	"	2	

* Personnel Trains consist of 48 covers and 2 officers' carriages - accommodation for approximately 1400 O.R. 50 men to a cover.

(a) Each Unit will detail sufficient loading party for their own transport and baggage. This should be as small as possible as accommodation on omnibus trains will be very limited.

(b) All Units will halt outside Station until order for entraining is given.

TABLE "B".

TRANSPORT AND BAGGAGE TRAINS.

Unit.	No. of Train.	No. of covers and flats.	Due at SOLINGEN Station GOODS ENTRANCE.	Due to leave SOLINGEN.	Station of arrival	No. of covers for Baggage.	Remarks.
Brigade H.Q.	No. 3	Covers 4 Flats 4	07.00 hours	10.19 hours	ROMERSKIRCHEN 13.20 hours.	3	Covers allotted for baggage include accommodation for loading personnel.
1st L.T.M.B.	"	-	"	"	"	1	
1/5th K.O.S.B.	"	WHOLE OF TRANSPORT BY ROAD VIA RHINE FERRY AT BENRATH				5	
51st H.L.I.	"	Covers 8 Flats 10	07.30 hours	10.19 hours	ROMERSKIRCHEN 13.30 hrs.	5	
15th H.L.I.	No. 4	Covers 8 Flats 10	10.00 hours	13.10 hours	ROMERSKIRCHEN 16.40 hrs.	5	
64 Fd. Coy. R.E.	"	Covers 7 Flats 7	10.30 "	"	"	4	Do.
28th Fd. Amb.	"	THE WHOLE TRANSPORT WILL GO BY ROAD VIA RHINE FERRY AT BENRATH				3	
105th Coy. RASC	"					2	

* Omnibus trains for Transport and Baggage consist of 1 coach, 30 covers and 17 flats. 6 H.D. or 8 other animals to a cover, or 30 men to one cover. The average flat takes 4 axles.

Appendix "A" *War Diary*

DISTRIBUTION.

No 1 Copy.	G.O.C.
2	Brigade Major.
3	Staff Captain.
4	Staff Captain (Civil Administration.)
5	Signal Officer.
6	Provost Officer.
7	Orderly Officer.
8	1/5th K.O.S.B.
9	15th H.L.I.
10	51st H.L.I.
11	1st Lowland Bde. T.M.B.
12	28th Field Ambulance.
13	105th Coy. R.A.S.C.
14	64th Field Coy. R.E.
15	Lowland Division "G"
16	Lowland Division "Q"
17	1st Light Brigade.
18	R.T.O. Opladen.
19	2nd Lowland Brigade.
20	3rd Lowland Brigade.
21, 22, & 23	File and Spare.
24 & 25	War Diary.

MOVE TO DORMAGEN AREA.

1st LOWLAND BRIGADE INSTRUCTIONS No 1.

Reference Maps.

   1 K 1/100,000
   2 K 1/100,000

8th July 1919.

1. RELIEF.

   The 1st Lowland Brigade Group will relieve the 1st Light Brigade in the Dormagen Area on 11th July 1919.

2. MOVE.

   Moves of both Personnel and Transport will be by rail, lorry and road in accordance with attached tables.

3. CIVIL ADMINISTRATION AND PROVOST OFFICE STAFF.

   The Civil Administration and Provost Office staff as detailed below will remain at SOLINGEN.

(a) <u>Civil Administration.</u>   (b) <u>Provost Staff.</u>

Capt. F. Leeves, M.C.,   Lieut. A. Ellis M.A.C.
  Staff Captain Civil   No 28529 Pte T. Nutters
  Administration.   1/5th K.O.S.B.
280343
  Sgt. B. Abrahams 15th H.L.I.
74247 Pte A. Morrison
  51st H.L.I.   Batman.
47133 Pte J. Colquhoun
  15th H.L.I.   Groom.

4. ADVANCED PARTIES /

(2)

4. ADVANCED PARTIES.

(a) Advanced Parties, strength as under, will move to 1st Light Brigade Area on 10th inst. for the purpose of taking over billeting accommodation etc. and for guiding Units to their billeting areas on arrival at DORMAGEN STATION.

UNIT	OFFICERS	O.R.s
Brigade Headquarters	1	4
1/5th K.O.S.B.	1	5
15th H.L.I.	1	5
51st H.L.I.	1	5
1st Lowland Bde. T.M.B.	1	1
105 Coy. R.A.S.C.	1	1
64th Field Coy. R.Es.	2x	2x
28th Field Ambulance	1	1
	9	24

x 1 to take over work shops and work at DORMAGEN.

The above will report at Brigade Headquarters at 09.30 hours on 10th inst. where lorries will be in readiness to convey them to new area. The senior officer will command the party.

The unconsumed portion of the day's rations and rations for 11th inst. will be taken. Kits and blankets will be taken.

(b) Advanced Parties, strength similar to those furnished by this Brigade Group will arrive in 1st Lowland Brigade Area from 1st Light Brigade on 10th inst.

They will be accommodated by Units whom they are relieving.

They will bring rations with them.

5. RELIEF of 51st H.L.I.

The relief of 51st H.L.I. in the line will be carried out by two Companies 18th K.R.R.C. on the evening of 10th inst.

The Companies 18th K.R.R.C. will arrive by lorries at Brigade Headquarters at 19.00 hours where a guide will conduct them to 51st H.L.I. Billets at FREDRICK STRASSE.

51st H.L.I. will provide the Companies with tea on arrival and afterwards they will be conveyed in the lorries to the Headquarters of the Companies in the line.

Relief will then be carried out and the Companies relieved will be conveyed back to SOLINGEN by the lorries.

1 Officer per Company and 1 N.C.O. per Post will remain in the line with the new Unit until 06.00 hours on 11th inst. when they will rejoin their Headquarters.

Copy of Brigade and Unit's Defence Scheme, Order Boards and any Instructions with reference to Perimeter Posts issued, will be handed over on relief.

Completion of relief will be wired to Brigade Headquarters.

(3)

6 GUARDS

(a) The 15th H.L.I. will furnish a Guard, strength 2 Officers, 2 Sergeants, 4 Corporals, 1 Bugler and 47 Other Ranks, on the DORMAGEN Factory, relieving a similar guard now furnished by 13th K.R.R.C.
This Guard will be formed from two complete Platoons if possible.
It will proceed by the 13.12 hours train from SOLINGEN STATION on 10th inst. changing at COLOGNE for DORMAGEN, and proceeding by the train for that Station arriving at 17.44 hours.

(b) 1/5th K.O.S.B. will furnish a Guard of one Section of not less than 1 N.C.O. and 6 Men from the Company to be quartered at STRUZELBERG, for the ST. PETERS CROSS ROADS POST, relieving a guard of 20th K.R.R.C.
The train arrangements for this Guard will be the same as for (a)
Rations for 10th and 11th will be taken by both Guards, also 1 Blanket per man and Officers' kits.
The 1st Light Brigade are being asked to provide transport to convey Officers' baggage from the Station to DORMAGEN.

(c) The permanent Guard at the STADTHAUS DETENTION ROOMS will be relieved by a Guard to be furnished by the Traffic Control Squadron at Retreat on 10th inst.

(d) Brigade Headquarters guard will march off at 12.00 hours on 11th inst. and will proceed to the new Area by the last troop train, due to leave SOLINGEN STATION at 13.00 hours. On arrival at DORMAGEN the guard will mount at Brigade Headquarters and will be relieved at Retreat in the usual way.

(e) The OHLIGS RAILHEAD GUARD will be relieved by a guard of 1st Light Brigade during the afternoon of 10th inst. On relief the relieved Guard will rejoin its Unit at SOLINGEN.

(f) The Guard on 104th Coy R.A.S.C. Ration Dump, OHLIGS, will not mount on 10th inst. as 104th Coy R.A.S.C. move on that date.

All boards of orders, Guard Room utensils, etc. will be handed over on relief.

7 LORRIES

Lorries will be provided as laid down in Table below. All stores which cannot be carried on these lorries or on the Horse Transport will be conveyed by rail.

Date	Time	No of Lorries	Reporting at	Load	Remarks.
July 10th	10.00 hours.	2	Bde. Hqrs.	Advance Party to DORMAGEN	Return to BEDBURG on completion
10th	18.00 hours	1	28th Field Ambulance.	Stores to Stn. only.	Report to Bde H.Q. on completion
10th	18.30 hours	2	1/5th K.O.S.B.	Stores	
10th	18.30 hours	2	15th H.L.I.	Stores	
10th	18.30 hours	2	51st H.L.I.	Stores	
10th	18.30 hours	1	105th Coy R.A.S.C. L.T.M.B.	Stores.	½ share to each Unit.
10th	18.30 hours	1	64th Coy R.E.	Stores	

These lorries except two for Advance Parties will be used to carry stores which are being sent by rail, to SOLINGEN Railway Station in the early morning of 11th inst., after which they will return to the Unit Headquarters, reload and rendezvous at Brigade Headquarters not later than 10.00 hours.

The minimum number of personnel for loading and unloading the stores will travel on the lorries.

The senior N.C.O. or man riding on each lorry will have written instructions as to where the stores are to be off loaded.

Lorries will not be overloaded. No replacements are available in the event of a breakdown.

All lorries will travel in a convoy and not singly.

They will only do one journey from SOLINGEN to DORMAGEN AREA.

The 51st H.L.I. will detail an officer to take charge of the lorry convoy when it rendezvous at Brigade Headquarters. On completion of the journey to DORMAGEN AREA and after off loading, all lorries will rendezvous at Brigade Headquarters, DORMAGEN and from there will proceed to their park at Bedburg.

In addition to above, one lorry will meet each personnel train at DORMAGEN STATION to convey cooking utensils and rations carried on the troop train, to the destinations of Units.

Other lorries will meet baggage trains at ROMMERSKIRCHEN to convey the baggage not loaded on Horse Transport, to the Units to which it belongs.

8. ENTRAINING AND EMBARKATION STATES.

(a) All Units will render Entraining States to Brigade Headquarters by 14.00 hours, 10th July, in the following form.

All baggage and supply wagons, their drivers and their animals will be shown on Units' Entraining States.

Officers	Animals		Vehicles	
	O.R.	H.D.	All other animals	4 wheeled	2 wheeled

(b) A State similar to above will be rendered for all personnel, animals and vehicles proceeding by ferry.

9. DUTIES.

The following officers will supervise the entraining, embarking, detraining and disembarking of the Brigade Group.

(a) At SOLINGEN — The Staff Captain, 1st Lowland Brigade, assisted by Capt. McNAUGHTON.

(b) At DORMAGEN — Lt. CAVE, Bde. Musketry Officer.

(c) At ROMMESKIRCHEN — An officer to be detailed by 15th H.L.I.

(d) At RHINE FERRY, DEFRATH — An officer to be detailed by 1/5th K.O.S.B.

(e) At RHINE FERRY, STURZELBERG — An officer to be detailed by 1/5th K.O.S.B.

With reference (b) and (c), the officers detailed will proceed by the first train to these stations.

Reference (d), the officer detailed will go to DEFRATH on 9th July to see the embarking of 2nd Brigade Transport at 10.00 hours, in order that he may see how the work is carried out. On the date of the move he will proceed to DEFRATH, reporting to the officer in charge of embarkation arrangements by 10.00 hours.

The officer detailed for duty at STURZELBERG will proceed across the Rhine on the first barge conveying Brigade Transport.

10. RETENTION ROOMS.

All soldiers in arrest confined in the STADTHAUS will be removed by the Unit to which the men belong by Retreat on 10th inst., after which time no further admission of men belonging to 1st Lowland Brigade will be made.

11. INSTITUTE EMPLOY.

The Troops employed at the Y.M.C.A., Salvation Army Canteen and SCOTTISH CHURCHES HUT will rejoin their Units after the Institute where they are employed closes on 10th inst. 1st Light Brigade are being asked to send other men in their place.

12. DOCUMENTS, etc., TO BE HANDED OVER.

Maps vide B.M./2(a)/707 of 6/7/19, copies of Defence Scheme, details regarding Training and Recreation facilities of the present Area will be handed over to and those for the new Area will be taken over from Units being relieved.

Units will also obtain at the same time copies of orders regarding Bathing now in force in the DORMAGEN AREA. These orders will remain in force pending the issue of Brigade Instructions on the subject.

Before any bathing is permitted Units will ensure that these orders are known and understood by all ranks. In the past several cases of drowning have occurred through men disregarding these orders.

13. AMMUNITION, etc.

All mobile reserves of S.A.A., Grenades and Trench Mortar Ammunition will be handed over to the Advance Parties of 1st Light Brigade and receipts in duplicate obtained, one copy of which will be forwarded to Brigade Headquarters. Similarly our Advance Parties will take over in the new Area from Units they relieve, the mobile reserve of S.A.A., Grenades and Trench Mortar Ammunition held by those Units, and will give to those Units a receipt for Ammunition, etc., taken over and send a copy of the receipt to Brigade Headquarters.

14. SURPLUS BRIGADE EMPLOY.

All N.C.O's and men employed at Brigade Headquarters who are not required in the new Area will be returned to duty at Retreat on 10th inst. Names of men being returned will be notified to Units as early as possible.

15. SUPPLIES.

Supply Railhead will remain at OHLIGS up to and including Thursday, 10th July. From 11th inst Railhead will be at BEDBURG.
Troops moving by train will entrain with the current days rations on the man or on the troop train. Rations for 12th inst. will be carried on the supply wagon which will move with Units. Rations for 13th inst. and afterwards will be delivered by lorry in the Area.
Transport moving by road will carry forage and rations for consumption on 11th inst.

16. BILLETS.

Billets will be handed over in a clean condition.
Units will hand over all requisitioned articles to the Unit relieving them. Receipts for all such articles handed over will be obtained in duplicate. One copy will be forwarded to Brigade Headquarters.

17. ORDNANCE STORES.

The Offices and Stores of D.A.D.O.S. are closed for the move. They will be reopened at LIPP on 11th inst.

18. CLEAN CLOTHING STORES.

The Clean Clothing Stores will be opened by the Baths Officer at BEDBURG on 11th inst.

19. TENTAGE.

Receipts in duplicate will be given and taken for all tentage handed over or taken over by Units. A copy of such receipts will be forwarded to Brigade Headquarters on completion of the move.

20. HANDING OVER OF COMMAND.

The Brigadier-General Commanding 1st Lowland Brigade will hand over the command of the Troops in, and the administration of No. 1 Sub-Area to the Lieut. Colonel Commanding 1st Light Brigade at 12.00 hours, 11th July, 1919.

(8)

21. LOCATION.

On arrival in the DORMAGEN AREA Units will be quartered as under:-

	Unit.	Place.	Relieving.
(a)	Brigade Headquarters	DORMAGEN	1st Light Bde H.Q.
(b)	15th H.L.I.	Do.	13th K.R.R.C.
(c)	51st H.L.I. H.Qrs.) 2 companies)	WORRINGEN	
	1 company in camp near FUHLINGEN		
	1 company	FUHLINGEN	18th K.R.R.C.
(d)	1/5th K.O.S.B. H.Qrs.) 3 companies)	ZONS	20th K.R.R.C.
	1 Company	STURZLEBERG	
(e)	64th Field Coy. R.E.	HORREM	20th Field Coy R.E.
(f)	28th Field Ambulance	SINNERSDORF	5th Field Ambnce.
(g)	105th Coy. R.A.S.C.	STRABERG	No. 3 Coy. Light Divisional Train.
(h)	1st Lowland Bde. L.T.M.B.	HACKENBORICH	1st Light T.M.B.

22. BRIGADE HEADQUARTERS.

Brigade Headquarters will close at SOLINGEN at 12.00 hours on 11th inst., and will reopen at DORMAGEN at 16.00 hours on same date.

Captain,
Brigade Major,
1st Lowland Brigade.

TABLE "A".

PERSONNEL TRAIN TABLE.

Unit.	No. of Train.	Nos. of Compts. and Covers for Personnel and Flats.	Time Units are due at SOLINGEN Station.	Time Train due to leave.	Station of arrival and time due.	Nos. of Covers for Baggage on No. 3 TRAIN.	Remarks
Brigade H.Q.	No. 1	2 compartments for officers 6 covers	07.20 hrs.	08.34 hrs.	DORMAGEN 11.54 hrs.	3	All surplus baggage for Units travelling on No. 1 Train moves with its loading parties on No. 3 Train to ROMERSKIRCHEN.
1st L.T.M.B.	No. 1	1 compartment 1 cover	07.20 "	"	"	1	
1/5th K.O.S.B.	No. 1	4 compartments 18 covers	07.25 "	"	"	5	
51st H.L.I.	No. 1	5 compartments 24 covers	07.40 "	"	"	5	
						TRAIN No. 4	
15th H.L.I.	No. 2	4 compartments 25 covers	07.55 "	09.08 "	DORMAGEN 12.17 hrs.	5	All surplus baggage for Units travelling on No. 2 Train moves with its loading party on No. 4 Train to ROMERSKIRCHEN.
54 Fd. Coy. R.E.	No. 2	1 compartment 5 covers	08.05 "	"	"	4	
28th Fd. Amb.	No. 2	1 compartment 3 covers	08.15 "	"	"	3	
105th Coy. RASC	No. 2	1 compartment	08.15 "	"	"	2	

* Personnel Trains consist of 48 covers and 2 officers' carriages - accommodation for approximately 1400 O.R. 50 men to a cover.

(a) Each Unit will detail sufficient loading party for their own transport and baggage. This should be as small as possible as accommodation on omnibus trains will be very limited.

(b) All Units will halt outside Station until order for entraining is given.

TABLE "B"

TRANSPORT AND BAGGAGE TRAINS.

Unit.	No. of Train.	No. of covers and flats.	Due at SOLINGEN Station GOODS ENTRANCE.	Due to leave SOLINGEN.	Station of arrival	No. of covers for Baggage.	Remarks.
Brigade H.Q.	No. 3	Covers 4 Flats 4	07.00 hours	10.19 hours	ROMMERSKIRCHEN 13.20 hours.	3	Covers allotted for baggage include accommodation for loading personnel.
1st L.T.M.B.	"	—	"	"	"	1	
1/5th K.O.S.B.	"	WHOLE OF TRANSPORT BY ROAD VIA RHINE FERRY AT BENRATH				3	
51st H.L.I.	"	Covers 6 Flats 10	07.30 hours	10.19 hours	ROMMERSKIRCHEN 13.20 hrs.	5	
15th H.L.I.	No. 4	Covers 8 Flats 10	10.00 hours	13.16 hours	ROMMERSKIRCHEN 16.40 hrs.	5	
64 Fd. Coy. R.E.	"	Covers 7 Flats 7	10.30 "	"	"	4	Do.
28th Fd. Amb.	"	THE WHOLE TRANSPORT WILL GO BY ROAD VIA RHINE FERRY AT BENRATH				3	
105th Coy. RASC	"					2	

* Omnibus Trains for Transport and Baggage consist of 1 coach, 30 covers and 17 flats. 6 H.D. or 8 other animals to a cover, or 30 men to one cover. The average flat takes 4 axles.

Appendix "B" War Diary

1st LOWLAND BRIGADE ORDER No 297

Reference Maps.
1 K 1/100,000
2 K 1/100,000
Solingen Sheet.

9-7-19.

1. Reference para 2 1st Lowland Brigade Instructions No 1 dated 5-7-19, the move of Transport by road will be in accordance with attached March Table.

2. The O.C. 105th Coy R.A.S.C. will command the column.

3. Animals will be watered and fed at LIERATH before embarking on the barge.

4. After crossing the ferry Units Transports will march independently to join their Headquarters.

5. Acknowledge.

W Carter
Captain,
Brigade Major,
1st Lowland Brigade.

DISTRIBUTION.

Copy No 1. G.O.C.
2. Brigade Major.
3. Staff Captain.
4. 1/5th K.O.S.B.
5. 29th Field Ambulance.
6. 105th Coy R.A.S.C.
7. Lowland Division "G"
8. Lowland Division "Q"
9. File.
10. Spare.
11. & 12. War Diary.

TABLE to accompany 1st LOWLAND BRIGADE ORDER No 207 dated 9-7-19.

Transport of Unit in Order of March.	Starting Point.	Time of passing.	Route.
1/5th K.O.S.B.	Cross Roads. HUNINGHEM E 15,33 on the SOLINGEN-OHLICS Road.	09.00 hours 11-7-19.	OHLICS - HIDEN FUSPATH.
23th Field Ambulance	Do	09.05 hours	Do
105th Coy. R.A.S.C.	Do	09.08 hours	Do

Appendix B
War Diary

1st LOWLAND BRIGADE ORDER No 297

Reference Maps.
   1 K 1/100,000
   2 K 1/100,000
   Solingen Sheet.

9-7-19.

1. Reference para 2 1st Lowland Brigade Instructions No 1 dated 5-7-19, the move of Transport by road will be in accordance with attached March Table.

2. The O.C. 105th Coy R.A.S.C. will command the column.

3. Animals will be watered and fed at BENRATH before embarking on the barge.

4. After crossing the ferry Units Transports will march independently to join their Headquarters.

5. Acknowledge.

W. Curtis
Captain,
Brigade Major,
1st Lowland Brigade.

DISTRIBUTION.

Copy No 1. G.O.C.
   2. Brigade Major.
   3. Staff Captain.
   4. 1/5th K.O.S.B.
   5. 89th Field Ambulance.
   6. 105th Coy R.A.S.C.
   7. Lowland Division "G"
   8. Lowland Division "Q"
   9. File.
  10. Spare.
  11. & 12. War Diary.

TABLE to accompany 1st LOWLAND BRIGADE ORDER No 207 dated 9-7-19.

Transport of Unit in Order of March.	Starting Point.	Time of passing.	Route.
1/5th K.O.S.B.	Cross Roads, LININGHOFEN F 15,83 on the SOLINGEN-OHLIGS Road.	09.00 hours 11-7-19.	OHLIGS - HILDEN BERPATH.
26th Field Ambulance	Do	09.05 hours	Do
105th Coy. R.A.S.C.	Do	09.08 hours	Do

Appendix "C"
War Diary

1st LOWLAND BRIGADE ORDER No. 298.

Reference Map
Germany 3(R) N.E. 20th July, 1919.
1/25,000

1.   1st Lowland Brigade Headquarters will move from DORMAGEN to HS. ARFF, O.5529, on Wednesday next, 23rd July, 1919.

2.   Civil Administrative and Provost Offices will remain at DORMAGEN.

3.   Brigade Headquarters will close at DORMAGEN at 10.00 hours on 23rd July, and will reopen at the same hour and date at H.S. ARFF.

W. Carter
Captain,
Brigade Major,
1st Lowland Brigade.

Copy. No. 1. Brigadier.
2. Brigade Major.
3. Staff Captain.
4. Staff Captain, Civil Administrative.
5. Provost Officer.
6. Signal Officer.
7. R.A.F., DORMAGEN.
8. Lowland Division (G)
9. Lowland Division (Q)
10. 2nd Lowland Brigade.
11. 3rd Lowland Brigade.
12. 105th Coy. R.A.S.C.
13. 64th Field Coy. R.E.
14. 28th Field Ambulance.
15. 1/5th K.O.S.B.
16. 15th H.L.I.
17. 51st H.L.I.
18. 1st Lowland Brigade L.T.M.B.
19. Spare.
20 & 21. War Diary.
22. File.

MOVE of BRIGADE HEADQUARTERS from
DORMAGEN to HS ARFF.

1. Brigade Headquarters is moving from DORMAGEN to HS ARFF on Wednesday next, 23rd inst.

2. The Brigade Signal Officer will arrange for opening up of Signal Communication before the move takes place.

    An exchange will be maintained at DORMAGEN and personnel will be left behind to man it.

3. All Civil Administration and Provost Office Staff (except Corporal Duncan) will remain at DORMAGEN.

4. The Staff Captain will arrange to send 30 Bell tents, complete with floor boards, and two marquees to the Football Field near the new Headquarters, which is the site chosen for the Camp.

    The tents and marquees will be drawn from those held by 1/5th K.O.S.B., and, if sufficient are not available then from D.A.D.O.S., Lowland Division.

    The Brigade Headquarters lorry will be detailed by the Staff Captain to report to Headquarters, 1/5th K.O.S.B. at 8.30 hours on Monday to convey tents to site of Camp, making as many journeys as necessary.

    1/5th K.O.S.B. will furnish loading parties.

    1st Lowland Brigade L.T.M.B. will unload the lorry at the site of the Camp and erect the tents. They will furnish a guard over the Camp until it is occupied on 23rd ins

    Lieut. CRIPPS will lay out the Camp. An officer to be detailed by O.C. Trench Mortar Battery will report to Lieut. CRIPPS at the Camp site at 08.30 hours on 21st to have the positions where the tents are to be erected pointed out to him.

5. The O.C. 64th Field Coy. R.E. will:-

    (a) Have the water pumping machinery at HS ARFF overhauled on Monday next.

    (b) Erect Latrines, Urinals, Wash places on the Camp site before 10.00 hours on 23rd inst.

    (c) Remove the Cookhouse at Brigade Headquarters, DORMAGEN, to the site of the Camp, and re-erect it there.

    (d) Build an oven near the new Cookhouse.

    An officer from 64th Field Coy. will meet Lieut. CRIPPS at the Camp site at 08.30 hours on 21st., when the last named officer will point out where the Cookhouses, etc are to be erected.

6.   The Staff Captain will arrange for any additional Transport required for the move.

7.   Lieut. CRIPPS will arrange for the formation of the personnel left behind at DORMAGEN into one mess.

The Staff Captain will arrange for the rationing of these men and also for the rationing of the 1st Light Brigade Farming personnel.

8.   Brigade Headquarters personnel will march to HS ARFF on 23rd July under the command of Lieut. CAVE. They will fall in in front of Brigade Headquarters and be ready to march off at 10.00 hours.

The Guard will march with Brigade Headquarters.

Dress - Marching Order. Steel helmets will be carried on the back of the pack.

9.   The Staff Captain, Civil Administrative, will arrange with Lieut. CRIPPS for the billeting of any part of Brigade Headquarters that cannot be accommodated at HS ARFF, either in the house or Camp.

W. Carter
Captain,
Brigade Major,
1st Lowland Brigade.

DISTRIBUTION.

Copy No.
1. B.O.O.
2. Brigade Major.
3. Staff Captain.
4. Brigade Signal Officer.
5. Staff Captain, Civil Administrative.
6. Provost Officer.
7. 1/5th K.O.S.B.
8. 1st Lowland Bde. L.T.M.B.
9. 64th Field Coy. R.E.
10. Lieut. Cave.
11. to 15. Spare.

Appendix C
War Diary

1st LOWLAND BRIGADE ORDER No. 298

Reference Map
Germany 5(R) N.E.
1/25,000

20th July, 1919.

1.   1st Lowland Brigade Headquarters will move from DORMAGEN to HS. ARFF, O.5529, on Wednesday next, 23rd July, 1919.

2.   Civil Administrative and Provost Offices will remain at DORMAGEN.

3.   Brigade Headquarters will close at DORMAGEN at 10.00 hours on 23rd July, and will reopen at the same hour and date at H.S. ARFF.

W. Carter
Captain,
Brigade Major,
1st Lowland Brigade.

Copy. No. 1. Brigadier.
2. Brigade Major.
3. Staff Captain.
4. Staff Captain, Civil Administrative.
5. Provost Officer.
6. Signal Officer.
7. R.A.F., DORMAGEN.
8. Lowland Division (G)
9. Lowland Division (Q)
10. 2nd Lowland Brigade.
11. 3rd Lowland Brigade.
12. 105th Coy. R.A.S.C.
13. 64th Field Coy. R.E.
14. 28th Field Ambulance.
15. 1/5th K.O.S.B.
16. 15th H.L.I.
17. 51st H.L.I.
18. 1st Lowland Brigade L.T.M.B.
19. Spare.
20 & 21. War Diary.
22. File.

MOVE of BRIGADE HEADQUARTERS from
DORMAGEN to HS ARFF.

War Diary

1. Brigade Headquarters is moving from DORMAGEN to HS ARFF on Wednesday next, 23rd inst.

2. The Brigade Signal Officer will arrange for opening up of Signal Communication before the move takes place.

   An exchange will be maintained at DORMAGEN and personnel will be left behind to man it.

3. All Civil Administration and Provost Office Staff (except Corporal Duncan) will remain at DORMAGEN.

4. The Staff Captain will arrange to send 30 Bell Tents, complete with floor boards, and two marquees to the Football Field near the new Headquarters, which is the site chosen for the Camp.

   The tents and marquees will be drawn from those held by 1/5th K.O.S.B., and, if sufficient are not available, then from D.A.D.O.S., Lowland Division.

   The Brigade Headquarters lorry will be detailed by the Staff Captain to report to Headquarters, 1/5th K.O.S.B. at 8.30 hours on Monday to convey tents to site of Camp, making as many journeys as necessary.

   1/5th K.O.S.B. will furnish loading parties.

   1st Lowland Brigade L.T.M.B. will unload the lorry at the site of the Camp and erect the tents. They will furnish a guard over the Camp until it is occupied on 23rd inst.

   Lieut. CRIPPS will lay out the Camp. An officer to be detailed by O.C. Trench Mortar Battery will report to Lieut. CRIPPS at the Camp site at 08.30 hours on 21st to have the positions where the tents are to be erected pointed out to him.

5. The O.C. 64th Field Coy. R.E. will:-

   (a) Have the water pumping machinery at HS ARFF overhauled on Monday next.

   (b) Erect Latrines, Urinals, Wash places on the Camp site before 10.00 hours on 23rd inst.

   (c) Remove the Cookhouse at Brigade Headquarters, DORMAGEN, to the site of the Camp, and re-erect it there.

   (d) Build an oven near the new Cookhouse.

   An officer from 64th Field Coy. will meet Lieut. CRIPPS at the Camp site at 08.30 hours on 21st., when the last named officer will point out where the Cookhouses, etc. are to be erected.

2.

6.   The Staff Captain will arrange for any additional Transport required for the move.

7.   Lieut. CRIPPS will arrange for the formation of the personnel left behind at DORMAGEN into one mess.

The Staff Captain will arrange for the rationing of these men and also for the rationing of the 1st Light Brigade Farming personnel.

8.   Brigade Headquarters personnel will march to HS ARFF on 23rd July under the command of Lieut. CAVE. They will fall in in front of Brigade Headquarters and be ready to march off at 10.00 hours.

The Guard will march with Brigade Headquarters.

Dress - Marching Order. Steel helmets will be carried on the back of the pack.

9.   The Staff Captain, Civil Administrative, will arrange with Lieut. CRIPPS for the billeting of any part of Brigade Headquarters that cannot be accommodated at HS ARFF, either in the house or Camp.

W. Carter
Captain,
Brigade Major,
1st Lowland Brigade.

DISTRIBUTION.

Copy No. 1. H.Q.C.
2. Brigade Major.
3. Staff Captain.
4. Brigade Signal Officer.
5. Staff Captain, Civil Administrative.
6. Provost Officer.
7. 1/5th K.O.S.B.
8. 1st Lowland Bde. L.T.M.B.
9. 64th Field Coy. R.E.
10. Lieut. Cave.
11. to 15. Spare.

ORIGINAL

WAR DIARY for August 1919
of
INTELLIGENCE SUMMARY.
(Erase heading not required.)

Army Form C. 2118.

Place	Date	Hour	Summary of Events and Information	Remarks and references to Appendices
H.S. ARFF	1/8/19		1st Lowland Brigade was quartered as follows on 1st August:-	
			Brigade Headquarters Hs. Arff 1/5th K.O.S.B. ZONS	
			15th H.L.I. DORMAGEN 51st H.L.I. WORRINGEN, FUHLINGEN and one	
			Company in Camp S.E. FUHLINGEN.	
			Company Training was continued by all Units until 15th August.	
	7/8/19		Brigade Order No 299 ordering the move of the 51st H.L.I. to STOMMEIN issued	Appendix A
	16/8/19		The period 16/8/19 to 16/9/19 was alloted for Company and Battalion Training B.M./4(H)/866 issued	Appendix B
			Brigade Stage of Rhine Army Championship Cross Country Run held at DORMAGEN winners 15th H.L.I.	
			Second 51st H.L.I. Third 1/5th K.O.S.B.	
			Brigade Stage of Rhine Army Championship Tug-of-War Light and Cathch Weight and athletic events held at DORMAGEN B.M./5(j)/904 attached	Appendix C

[signature]
Brigadier-General,
Commanding 1st Lowland Brigade.

1st LOWLAND BRIGADE ORDER No 299

Appendix A

Reference Map:-

Germany, Sheet 59 1/200000 COLOGNE

7th August 1919.

1. The 51st H.L.I. will move to STOMMEIN tomorrow, 8th August, relieving 11th Royal Scots whose Billets they will occupy.

2. No restrictions as regards roads.

3. Move to be completed by 13.00 hours.

4. 4 Lorries will report to Battalion Headquarters, WORRINGEN at 07.30 hours on the 8th for conveyance of extra baggage and stores.

   The two baggage waggons belonging to Unit and one additional G.S. Waggon to be detailed by 105 Coy R.A.S.C. will report at Battalion Headquarters at 08.00 hours same date.

5. The Staff Captain, Civil Administration, will notify Unit as to disposal of requisitioned and hired stores.

6. All tents held on charge by 51st H.L.I. will be struck and returned to D.A.D.O.S. in the lorries used for conveyance of baggage. A loading and handing over party will be provided by the Unit.

   Palliasses not required at STOMMEIN will be returned to D.A.D.O.S. by the lorries. These will be returned empty.

7. All work on cook-houses and latrines, etc. now being done by 11th Royal Scots at STOMMEIN will be taken over by 51st H.L.I. and completed as early as possible.

   Acknowledge.

                                        Captain,
                                    Brigade Major,
                                   1st Lowland Brigade.

DISTRIBUTION

No. 1 G.O.C.
" 2 Brigade Major
" 3 Staff Captain
" 4 Staff Captain, (Civil Administration)
" 5 Signal Officer.
" 6 15th H.L.I.
" 7 51st H.L.I.
" 8 1/5th K.O.S.B.
" 9 1st Lowland Brigade T.M.B.
" 10 Lowland Division 'G'
" 11 Lowland Division 'Q'
" 12 2nd Lowland Brigade
" 13 105 Coy R.A.S.C.
" 14 28th Field Ambulance
" 15 64th Field Coy. R.E.
" 16 Brigade Supply Officer.

1/5th K.O.S.B.
15th H.L.I.
51st H.L.I.
Lowland Division (for Information)

No B.M./4(H)/866   10th August 1919.

     With reference to G.H.Q. letter No G.T.76 dated 20th May 1919, forwarded under B.M./4(H)/362 para. 7 the period alloted to Battalion and Brigade Training, 16th August to 15th September, will be utilized by Battalions in Battalion and Company Training.

     This change is rendered necessary owing to the limited extent of training ground available in the Brigade area, the only training ground of sufficient size for a Battalion operation being that situated between Natchijall and St Peters Post on both sides of the DORMAGEN NEUSS Road. This ground is re-alloted for the period as shown on attached sheet.

     The Brigade Commander realizes that owing to lack of training ground it will not be possible to carry out Battalion Training in its entirety, particularly in the case of 51st H.L.I. but he wishes that at least two days per week should be devoted to Battalion exercises in order that the control of the Unit by the Commanding Officers and co-operation between Companies, so necessary to success in action, may be practised.

     Every opportunity should be taken to carry out regimental exercises without troops, on some of the days when the Battalion ground is not alloted to the Unit.

     Copies of all Battalion Exercises (with or without troops) will be forwarded to Brigade Headquarters 48 hours before the exercise is to be carried out.

                                                      Captain,
                                             Brigade Major,
                                        1st Lowland Brigade.

Allotment of Training Ground on the

DORMAGEN - NEUSZ Road.
=================

18th August   )
19th   "   )   1/5th K.O.S.B.
20th   "   )

21st August   )
22nd August   )   15th H.L.I.
23rd August   )

25th August   )
26th   "   )   1/5th K.O.S.B.
27th   "   )

28th   "   )
29th   "   )   15th H.L.I.
30th   "   )

Appendix C

1/5th K.O.S.B.
15th H.L.I.
51st H.L.I.
1st Lowland Brigade T.M.B.
Camp Commandant.

B.M./5(J)/804   21st August 1919.

1. In continuance of my B.M./5(D)/880 dated 13th August it is notified for information that the Divisional Stage of the Rhine Army Championship is not now being held vide notice in D.R.O. dated 18th August 1919.

2. The 1st Lowland Brigade Stage will be held as arranged, on Monday 25th August on the 15th H.L.I. Recreation Ground beginning at 2 p.m.

3. Medals will be given for the winning Cross Country Team, Catch Weight Tug of War and Light Weight Tug of War Teams as well as for the Athletic Events.

4. The prizes will be purchased from funds provided by units according to their ration strengths and from the Brigade Games Fund.

5. The Band of the 9th East Surrey Regt. 1st London Brigade has been lent for the occasion.

6. Each unit will provide tea for their Officers and for their own men, both competitors and spectators.
Brigade Headquarters and Trench Mortar Battery will provide two Officers Tea tents. The 15th H.L.I. have been asked to provide the Brass Band with dinner and tea.
15th H.L.I. will lend each unit a field cooker.

7. Marquees are being erected on the ground and are alloted as follows:-

    2   Brigade Headquarters and Trench Mortar Battery.
    1   1/5th K.O.S.B.
    1   15th H.L.I.
    1   51st H.L.I.
    1   For use of the Band.
    1   15th H.L.I. for canteen.

Two Bell Tents will be pitched for each Battalion for dressing purposes.

8. The 15th H.L.I. have consented to open a canteen on the ground for the sale of minerals and beer and also cigarettes and chocolates if a special allotment can be made. The profits from this canteen are being paid into the Brigade Sports Fund.

9. The Sports ground is being prepared under the direction of C.S.M. Johnson, Brigade P.&.T.S. Instructor.
15th H.L.I. are providing the necessary working parties and arranging for the cutting of the grass.

10. The flags, hurdles, ropes and other impediments required for the ground are being lent by 15th H.L.I. and No. 1 A.D., R.A.F.

11.   Lorries have been asked for as follows:-

2 to convey Band of East Surrey Regt. to and from their their quarters.

10 for 51st H.L.I. 1 from 8.0 a.m. to convey foodstuffs, etc., required for teas.
9 for conveying competitors and spectators from 11 a.m.

2 for 1/5th K.O.S.B. from 8.0 a.m. to convey foodstuffs for tea, and competitors, etc.

1 for 15th H.L.I. from 8.0 a.m. for foodstuffs for tea.

3 for 1st Lowland Brigade Headquarters and T.M.B. from 8.0 a.m. for foodstuffs and competitors, etc.

12.   Light Tug-of-War teams will be weighed on the ground. A Judge will superintend the weighing in.

13.   Units are requested to ask their expert clowns to attend and amuse the spectators.

14.   Each Battalion will detail a Company Sergeant Major to be in charge of their Dressing Tents. These Warrant Officers should be made responsible that the Competitors are dressed and on the course one event ahead.

Captain,
Brigade Major,
1st Lowland Brigade.

BRIGADE ROUTINE ORDERS
by
Brigadier-General G.T.C. CARTER-CAMPBELL, C.B., D.S.O.,
Commanding 1st Lowland Brigade.

No 440   Tuesday, 26th August 1919.

No orders were issued on August 24th and 25th.

Part 1.

126 BRIGADE SPORTS MEETING

The following are the results of the 1st Lowland Brigade Sports held at DORMAGEN on the 25th.inst:-

	First.	Second
880 Yards Flat Race	2/Lt Barrowcliffe, 1/5th K.O.S.B.	R.Q.M.S. Tinckler 1/5th K.O.S.B.
High Jump	Capt. Russell 51st H.L.I.	Sergt Chisholm 51st H.L.I.
440 Yards Flat Race	Sergt May 51st H.L.I.	Pte Daniels 15th H.L.I.
Long Jump	Sgt. Chisholm 51st H.L.I.	Capt. Stevenson 51st H.L.I.
1 Mile Flat Race	2/Lt Barrowcliffe 1/5th K.O.S.B.	R.Q.M.S. Tinckler 1/5th K.O.S.B.
Putting the Shot	Sgt McColl 51st H.L.I.	G.S.M. Shorten 51st H.L.I.
1 Mile Relay Race	1/5th K.O.S.B.	51st H.L.I.
100 Yards Flat Race	Pte Daniels 15th H.L.I.	Capt Russell 51st H.L.I.
3 Miles Flat Race	R.Q.M.S. Tinckler 1/5th K.O.S.B.	Pte Rooney 15th H.L.I.
120 Yards Hurdle Race	Capt Russell 51st H.L.I.	Pte Brown 15th H.L.I.
Sack and Boot Race	Pte Wilson 15th H.L.I.	Pte Borland L.T.M.B.
Boat Race	1/5th K.O.S.B.	
Squad Drill Blindfolded	51st H.L.I.	
Victoria Cross Race on Mules	Dr Findlay 1/5th K.O.S.B.	Dr S. Anderson 15th H.L.I.
Band Race	L/Cpl Walsh 9th East Surrey Regt	Pte Knight 9th East Surrey Regt

Light/

2.

	First	Second
Light Weight Tug-of-War	51st H.L.I.	
Catch Weight Tug-of-War	15th H.L.I.	

Army Championship Points:-

    51st H.L.I.   38 Points
    1/5th K.O.S.B. 33 "
    15th H.L.I.   27 "

[signature]

Captain,
Brigade Major,
1st Lowland Brigade.

Part 2

500 **DEMOBILIZATION**

Cases of personnel referred to in Corps Routine Order 165 will be referred to Brigade Headquarters.

501 **RETURN**

The Return called for in G.R.O. 3217 will be forwarded to Brigade Headquarters by 14.00 hours on 2nd of each month.

[signature]

Captain,
Staff Captain,
1st Lowland BRigade.

ORIGINAL

1st LOWLAND BRIGADE HEADQUARTERS

WAR DIARY

FOR

SEPTEMBER 1919

Army Form C. 2118.

WAR DIARY

~~INTELLIGENCE SUMMARY~~

(Erase heading not required.)

Instructions regarding War Diaries and Intelligence Summaries are contained in F. S. Regs., Part II. and the Staff Manual respectively. Title pages will be prepared in manuscript.

Place	Date	Hour	Summary of Events and Information	Remarks and references to Appendices
HS ARFF	18th Sept.		Orders received from Lowland Division for 1/5th Kings Own Scottish Borderers to be reduced to Cadre and to proceed to the United Kingdom with 8th K.O.S.B.	A
"	20th	"	1st Lowland Brigade Order No. 301 issued. No. 300 was issued and cancelled	Appendix A.
"	22nd	"	Telegraphic Instructions received for 1st Lowland Brigade T.M.B. to be reduced to Cadre.	B
"	23rd	"	1st Lowland Brigade Order No. 302 issued	Appendix B.
"	24th	"	1st Lowland Brigade T.M.B. reduced to Cadre as from this date.	W
"	"	"	Orders received from Lowland Division that 1st Lowland Brigade H. Qrs. be disbanded as from 12.00 hours, 25/9/19. 1st Lowland Brigade Order No. 303 issued	Appendix C.
			The Disposal of Staff Officers on disbandment were as follows:-	
			Brigadier — Brig.-Gen. G.T.C. CARTER-CAMBELL, C.B., D.S.O., To England preparatory to assuming the command of a Brigade in Ireland.	W
			Brigade Major — Capt. W. CARTER, D.S.O., M.C. To 3rd Southern Brigade as Bde. Major.	W
			Staff Captain — Capt. E.R. SALTONSTALL, M.C.	
			Education Officer — Capt. J.P. McNAUGHTON. To 15th W.L.I. pending further	
			C. of E. Chaplain — Rev. A.E. MORRIS. ditto	
			Brigade Signal Officer Lt. R.T. CRIPPS — Rejoins Division Signal Coy. H.Q.	
	25th		Special Order of the Day. [signature] Brigadier-General, Commanding 1st Lowland Brigade.	Appendix D

War Diary

1st LOWLAND BRIGADE ORDER No 301.

20/9/19.

1. 1st Lowland Brigade Order No 300 dated 14/9/19 and No B. ./11/981 dated 17th September containing further instructions regarding move of 1/5th K.O.S.B. areas ncelled and the following substituted.

2. The following Units belonging to the Lowland Division are being despatched to the United Kingdom on 25th September 1919.
    1/4th Royal Scots Fusiliers.
    5th Bn. Kings Own Scottish Borderers.
    15th Bn. Highland Light Infantry.

3. The 1/5th Bn. Kings Own Scottish Borderers will be reduced to Cadre and accompany 5th Bn. Kings Own Scottish Borderers to the United Kingdom. Strength of Cadre to be 4 Officers and 35 Other Ranks. Cadre to be composed of demobilizable personnel.

4. Volunteers and retainable men will be transferred to 5th K.O.S.B. and with the Cadre will proceed to join that battalion on 22nd September. The Cadre and other personnel will proceed from DOPHACEN to DUREN by passenger trains, one half at 07.07 hours, the remainder by the train leaving at 11.25 hours.
    On arrival at Duren they will come under the orders of Brigadier Commanding 2nd Lowland Brigade.
    The 1/5th K.O.S.B. will detail an Officer to assist the R.T.O. DO....... Station with the entraining. He should proceed to Duren by the second train.

5. Personnel other than Cadre (if any) of 1/5th K.O.S.B. (except Transport men) elegible for demobilization will proceed to Duren on 22nd September and report to O.C. 2nd Lowland Brigade Demobilization Camp.

6. Any Officer or other Ranks left behind who are not elegible for demobilization will be dealt with in accordance with G.R.O. 2987. Rolls in accordance with G.R.O. 3584 para 5 will be submitted to G.H.Q. by 1/5th K.O.S.B. on 25th September.

7. Transport of 1/5th K.O.S.B. together with their supply and baggage waggons will move to BEDBURG by road on 21st September rationed and foraged for consumption on 22nd and 23rd September. 15th H.L.I. will provide any extra animals required. These will be at ZONS by 9.0 hours 21st inst. Any route may be followed.
    4th Royal Scots Fusiliers is providing billets for night of 21st and 22nd.

8. The vehicles and equipment, other than personnel equipment, 1/5th K.O.S.B. will be entrained at HARFF Station on 23rd.
    The C.R.A. is providing animals to complete turnout. These animals will be at Headquarters 4th R.S.F. at 10.30 hours 23rd September to draw vehicles to Harff Station.
    Personnel equipment will accompany Unit.

(2)

9. The 1/4th R.S.F. and 1/5th K.O.S.B. have been allotted to No 1 Equipment Train. Load up at HARFF Station at 12.00 hours, depart 13.23 hours 23rd September.

10. The 4th R.S.F. is providing a loading party of 100 men which will be at Harff Station at 12.00 hours on 23rd September.

11. The 1/5th K.O.S.B. will detail 1 Officer, 1 C.Q.M.S. and 6 men to accompany the Equipment Train.

12. The destination in United Kingdom of the Transport and Stores is C.O.O. CHIDWELL via ANTWERP.

13. All animals belonging to 1/5th K.O.S.B. will be handed over to the Lowland Division Artillery on 23rd September. Animals lent by 15th H.L.I. (vide para 5) will return to their Unit on 23rd September.

14. Transport personnel 1/5th K.O.S.B. after handing over their animals will proceed to Duren by passenger train from BEDBURG Station. Retainable men report to 6th K.O.S.B, remainder to Demobilization Camp at DUREN BARRACKS.

15. The 1/5th K.O.S.B. will send a billeting Officer to Duren to make the necessary arrangements for accommodation of Unit on arrival.

16. Attention is directed to Lowland Division No Q 252 dated 18th August 1919 and subsequent amendments which will be complied with. Special attention is directed to Lowland Division Q 252/36 dated 28th August 1919.

17. The Cadre 1/5th K.O.S.B. will proceed with 6th K.O.S.B. from DUREN Station on 25th inst. Train programme will be notified later.

18. Ration arrangements are as follows:-
(a) Cadre 1/5th K.O.S.B. and personnel for transfer to 6th K.O.S.B. and those mentioned in para 5 will take with them the unconsumed rations for the 22nd inst. Rations for 23rd will be collected by the Battalion at DORMAGEN Station before the departure of 2nd Train and conveyed on that Train. Rations for 24th will be supplied by S.O. 2nd Brigade. Train rations for journey to U.K. will be supplied by 2nd Brigade.
(b) Transport animals will be foraged by Lowland Division Artillery on 24th.
(c) Iron rations, one per man will be drawn by 1/5th K.O.S.B. from S.O. 1st Lowland Brigade on 21st inst.

ACKNOWLEDGE.

W Carter
Captain,
Brigade Major,
1st Lowland Brigade.

DISTRIBUTION.

```
Copy No  1   G.O.C.
         2   Brigade-Major
         3   Staff Captain
         4   Staff Captain (Civil Duties)
         5   Signal Officer.
         6   1/5th K.O.S.B.
         7   15th H.L.I.
         8   51st H.L.I.
         9   1st Lowland Bde. T.M.B.
        10   R.T.O. DORMAGEN.
        11   Lowland Divn. Artillery.
        12   No 2 Coy. Divisional Train.
        13   Brigade Supply Officer.
        14   64th Field Coy. R.E.
        15   Lowland Division G
        16   Lowland Division Q
        17 & 18 War Diary.
        19   File.
        20   Provost Officer.
        21   2nd Lowland Brigade.
        22 & 23 Spare.
```

1st LOWLAND BRIGADE ORDER No. 302.

23rd September, 1919.

1. The Personnel at present employed with the 1st Lowland T.M.B. will rejoin their Battalions for duty by 12.00 hours tomorrow, 24th inst.

2. O.C. 1st Lowland T.M.B. will check carefully all stores and equipment: these will be handed in to Brigade Headquarters by 10.00 hours tomorrow.

1 N.C.O. will be left in charge of these stores: he will be attached to Brigade Headquarters for rations and discipline.

List of stores in triplicate will be forwarded to Brigade Headquarters, also lists showing deficiencies (is any).

The Brigade lorry will report to O.C. T.M.B. at 09.00 hours to convey stores to Brigade Headquarters.

All documents and books will be forwarded to Brigade Headquarters along with stores.

3. Rations for this personnel for 25th, 26th and 27th will be transferred to the Units concerned at the refilling point, after which date they will be shown on the Units' A.F. B.55.

The following are the numbers rejoining:-

    15th H.L.I.   1 officer   22 O.R.
    51st H.L.I.   -   22 "

(sgd) E.R. SALTONSTALL, Captain,
for Brigade Major,
1st Lowland Brigade.

DISTRIBUTION.

Copy. No. 1   B.G.C.
        2   Brigade Major.
        3   Staff Captain.
        4   1st Lowland L.T.M.B.
        5   15th H.L.I.
        6   51st H.L.I.
        7   No. 2 Coy. R.A.S.C.
        8   Brigade Q.M.S.
        9   Lowland Division "G".
       10   Lowland Division "Q".

War Diary

1st LOWLAND BRIGADE ORDER No. 303.

24th September, 1919.

1. The Headquarters of 1st Lowland Brigade will be disbanded at 12 noon, 25th September, 1919.

2. Lieut.-Colonel A.B. THORBURN, 15th Bn. H.L.I., will take over the duties of Area Commandant, DORMAGEN Sub-Area, at above mentioned hour and date.

3. On the disbandment of 1st Lowland Brigade Headquarters

   (a) 15th and 51st Bn. Highland Light Infantry will become Divisional troops.

   (b) 1st Lowland Brigade Trench Mortar Battery, reduced to Cadre, will move to DUREN tomorrow at 09.00 hours, reporting at Divisional Store, DUREN Barracks.

   (c) 1st Lowland Brigade Signal Section will rejoin its Company Headquarters on Sunday, 28th inst., under orders to be issued by the Officer Commanding.

   (d) N.C.Os and men borne on the establishment of Brigade Headquarters will be dispersed on 27th inst. under instructions issued separately.

   (e) The Headquarters Mobilization Equipment will be handed in to D.A.D.O.S. on 25th inst.

   (f) Transport will be handed over to 105th Coy. R.A.S.C. on 25th inst.

4. The Brigade Baths at DORMAGEN will be taken over by 15th H.L.I. from 26th inst.

5. All officers and other ranks employed on Civil Police Duties will be attached to 15th Bn. Highland Light Infantry from 25th inst., and rationed from 29th.

6. Troops of the 1st Light Brigade at DORMAGEN will be attached to 15th H.L.I. from 25th inst., rationed from 29th inst.

ACKNOWLEDGE.

Captain,
Brigade Major,
1st Lowland Brigade.

DISTRIBUTION.

    Copy No. 1   G.O.C.
             2   Brigade Major.
             3   Staff Captain.
             4   Staff Captain, Civil Administration.
             5   Brigade Signal Officer.
             6   Provost Officer, DORMAGEN.
             7   15th H.L.I.
             8   51st H.L.I.
             9   64th Field Coy. R.E.
            10   105th Coy. R.A.S.C.
            11   Lowland Division "G".
            12   Lowland Division "Q".
            13   Lieut.-Colonel THORBURN.
            14   1st Light Brigade Farm.
      15 & 16   War Diary.
            17   File.
      18 & 19   Spare.

Appendix D.

SPECIAL ORDER OF THE DAY.

HS. ARFF.   25th September, 1919.

On giving up command of the 1st Lowland Brigade I wish to express to all Ranks my appreciation of their soldierly spirit and bearing while under my command.   I feel confident that should the necessity for active operations have arisen all ranks of the 1st Lowland Brigade would have acquitted themselves as Scotchmen have invariably done throughout the War.

[signature]

Brigadier-General,
Commanding 1st Lowland Brigade.

www.ingramcontent.com/pod-product-compliance
Lightning Source LLC
Chambersburg PA
CBHW081429160426

43193CB00013B/2228